32 great bible studies for youth

By Keith Stulp

CRC Publications
Reformed Church Press
Youth Unlimited

CRC Publications thanks Keith Stulp for writing this course for high school students. Stulp is a high school teacher, coach, and Young Life leader from Grand Rapids, Michigan.

Unless otherwise specified, Scripture quotations in this publication are from the HOLY BIBLE, NEW INTERNATIONAL VERSION, © 1973, 1977, 1984, International Bible Society. Used by permission of Zondervan Bible Publishers.

Scripture quotations from THE MESSAGE, © 1993, 1994, 1995, are used by permission of NavPress Publishing Group.

Illustrations on pages 15 and 16 by Matt VanderPol.

32 Great Bible Studies for Youth by Keith Stulp. Youth group and church school material for grades 9-12. © 1998, CRC Publications, 2850 Kalamazoo Ave. SE, Grand Rapids, MI 49560. All rights reserved. Printed in the United States of America on recycled paper. ♻ 1-800-333-8300

ISBN 1-56212-349-1

10 9 8 7 6 5 4 3 2

Contents

User's Guide

32 Great Bible Studies for Youth offers photocopiable, one-page Bible studies on topics of interest to high school youth. The material is simple to use, complete, and biblically responsible. Using a straightforward approach, it treats high schoolers as responsible young adults who want to learn more about the Bible and its meaning for their lives. Its goal is to help them practice that Word in their daily living.

32 Great Bible Studies is readily adaptable to a variety of settings and uses. The course is available in both print and electronic format. *32 Great Bible Studies for Youth* is a joint publication of CRC Publications, Reformed Church Press, and Youth Unlimited.

WHERE TO USE THESE STUDIES

Student-led Groups

32 Great Bible Studies for Youth was written especially for student-led groups of high schoolers who are conducting their own Bible study without the direct supervision of adult leaders. You'll want to read author Keith Stulp's comments on using this material for that purpose—please see page 9 of this book.

Student-led Bible study groups are becoming increasingly popular in high schools, youth group meetings, retreats, and other settings. Adult leaders of such groups usually work with student leaders (of small groups), helping them select materials, plan their meetings, and handle any problems or special needs. Typically, adult leaders also convene the various small groups into large-group meetings.

If you are working with student-led groups, you'll find a handout called **Instructions for Student-led Groups,** which you can photocopy and give to small group leaders. They, in turn, can give it to their group members, if they wish. See page 13.

Student-led small groups usually work best with five to ten students in each small group.

Youth Groups

If you are looking for high-quality Bible studies for your youth group that require minimal preparation for you as an adult leader, these materials will serve you well.

Within your youth group, you might do the Warm-up questions with the whole group, then break into smaller groups for the Bible study itself, and finish by returning to the large group for the Group Talk discussion questions at the end of each study. Or, if you prefer, walk with the kids through the entire study.

Each Bible study will take from thirty-five to sixty minutes, depending on how many of the questions you use and the extent of your discussion.

Retreats

Planning a retreat is a lot easier once you've selected a theme or topic on which to focus. Check out the topics of the various units in this course, then use the Bible studies from one unit—say "Decisions" or "Stressors"—as the core of your retreat. Build your retreat around the studies, letting kids run their own small group Bible studies. Supplement the studies with topic-related activities, games, guest speakers, recreational time, and so on.

Church School

High schoolers in church school settings often need a break from longer blocks of curriculum. Slip in a short unit from *32 Great* on gossip or service or stressors or relationships. Maybe let teens run all or part of their own Bible studies. Or supplement a regular curriculum unit on one of these topics with some additional Bible studies. Or (if it goes over well), try *32 Great* for a semester or even longer.

FORMAT

There are 32 Bible studies from which you can choose (plus a start-up meeting). The studies are clustered in units ranging from two to six meetings each. The units cover topics like decisions, gossip, fear, stressors, relationships, and more. It doesn't matter what order you take the units in, but once you and the group choose a topic, you'll probably want to take the meetings within that topic in sequence.

Each Bible study is complete on two sides of a single page. Don't feel that you have to discuss every question on these sheets. If a question bombs, drop it and move on to the next one. If a question produces some good talk, stay with it for a while. Going through all the questions will probably take your group at least forty-five minutes.

Meetings should begin with the **Warm-up** questions. Please note that although the questions are in the right-hand column, they should be read first, before the introductory comments. The first question is just an icebreaker meant to get the group talking to each other. It may or may not have anything to do with the topic. The second and third questions should definitely nudge the group toward the theme of the meeting.

After the warm-up questions, have group members take turns reading the **introductory comments** in the left-hand column. The comments are meant to introduce the topic and the Bible study on side two.

On side two you'll find **Scripture** and six related **questions.** Before reading Scripture, have someone read question 1—it will give the group something to look for while reading. Questions 1-3 get at important facts in the passage. Questions 4-6 interpret and apply the passage. Question 6 is especially important because it asks teens to personalize the Bible study and to practice (during the week) what they learned. Author Keith Stulp says, "I encourage— and encourage and encourage—my student leaders to buy a notebook and keep track of how people respond to question 6. That way, at the next meeting, leaders and their groups can talk about how things went that week. I believe it's very important for teens to realize that just getting together for Bible study isn't enough; it's practicing their faith that counts."

The **Group Talk** questions at the end raise some additional important "real-life" issues and problems that are related to the topic. They offer a good format for group members to give each other practical help and advice.

START-UP MEETING

You may want to use the optional handout "The Crest Thing" for your start-up meeting (see p. 15). It's strictly for letting kids get to know each other a little better. It's not a Bible study, so it doesn't count as one of the 32 in this book!

Please feel free to contact CRC Publications with your comments or questions about *32 Great Bible Studies for Youth* (you may also contact the author directly—see p. 11 for his e-mail address). Our hope and prayer is that these materials will be useful to you in your ministry with high school youth.

Bob Rozema
Curriculum Editor
CRC Publications
1-800-333-8300

Author's Comments on Using 32 Great with Student-Led Groups

The contents of this book were created for a high school Bible study group—called Young Life Campaigners—held at South Christian High School in Grand Rapids, Michigan. Once a week for the past six years, students have met at 7:00 a.m. in the library of the school and have used these resources in small group Bible study. While the format of the study initially was developed by two ministers, it has been greatly modified at the request of the seniors who run the small groups.

One goal of these Bible study sheets has been to enable a group of high school students to complete a topical Bible study without the direct supervision of adult leaders.

God has blessed the Campaigner ministry at South Christian. For the last several years, there have been twenty to twenty-five small groups with between 150 to 200 students attending. As leaders, we supply donuts for the groups (group members bring three dollars for the year) and then spend time in "big group" singing. We also listen to "big group" praises and prayer requests.

After about fifteen or twenty minutes, the groups split up and do the Bible studies. The student leaders know they have wide latitude within their groups. For example, if a member of the group has been through a traumatic experience, the group may need to spend time addressing that need.

I've found that the photocopied handouts usually have much more material than the groups can cover in the thirty-five minutes that are available. So I usually place the studies in the lockers of student leaders one or two days before the meeting. That way they can spend some devotional time with the material and decide what parts of the study they want to use. I firmly tell my leaders never to cut back on reading Scripture in their group meetings and always to spend time praying for each other (our group members often hold hands while praying). Everything else is ancillary.

While adults often lead the big group meeting, students do too, playing guitars and taking turns leading devotions. It's been my experience that the more you expect and encourage students to be involved, the more invested they become.

Each month I have the leaders over for dinner at my house to hang out and to check in. If there are any issues or ideas to discuss, it takes place then. What has become a bit of a mantra in this ministry for me is to remind the student leaders that I am there to serve them and that it is *their* ministry to run for their fellow students.

Choosing leaders is a difficult process and probably never done quite right. I use high school seniors as my small group leaders. We look at where we believe seniors are spiritually and how much experience they have in Campaigners. We also look to see how involved they are in their churches and how they interact socially. We try very hard never to set someone up to fail. Given the choice between someone who is a charismatic leader and someone who, while not as dynamic, is more spiritually mature, we opt for the latter. We also ask seniors to fill out a form, which basically asks why they want to be a leader and what qualifies them.

Ultimately, after we have chosen one leader per group, we place the other applicants with leaders, who are instructed to share the leadership with these people. The problem we face, of course, is trying to be as inclusive as possible while not damaging the integrity of the group by appointing a leader who will not lead positively, either inside the group or by his or her lifestyle.

I believe the Spirit has worked positively at South Christian through these Bible study groups. What has made the groups work—besides the great blessing of God—has been our commitment to giving students permission to lead themselves and to give their own direction to the groups.

I have been involved in this ministry for ten years now. Students can count on the meetings happening on schedule. The standards have not wavered. I believe that it's important to give our young people—who have so much change in their lives—something they can depend on.

We also try to make this a place where young people feel secure. It is not a place where put-downs are allowed (beyond the obvious and familiar type among friends). When someone shares in our big group meeting, the person first has to say "My name is ____." And everyone replies, "Hi, ____!" before the person continues. It's like a big AA meeting! It is very important that the Bible study does not become a place for "those kind of people." Everyone must be gladly accepted and made to feel welcome.

Many people have helped with the writing of these studies, both by giving ideas and by offering critique and editorial comments. I especially want to thank the many students at South Christian who cared enough about their Lord and their fellow students to make this Bible study a reality.

I value your questions and comments (and especially your ideas!). I can be reached at Flashkeith@aol.com.

Please let me know if I can be of service to you. Thanks.

In Christ's service,
Keith ("Flash") Stulp

Instructions for Student-Led Groups

Welcome to Bible study time! If you're reading this, I'll assume you're part of a group of high school students who are studying the Bible without the supervision of an adult leader. That's how my Young Life groups used these studies.

There are 32 Bible studies from which you can choose (plus a start-up meeting). The studies are clustered around topics like decisions, gossip, fear, stressors, relationships, and more. It doesn't matter what order you take the topics in, but once you choose a topic, you'll generally want to take the meetings within that topic in sequence.

Each Bible study is complete on two sides of a single page. Just photocopy and use. No further equipment or knowledge needed. Don't feel that you have to discuss every last question on these sheets. If a question bombs, drop it and move on to the next one. If a question produces some good talk, stay with it for a while.

I suggest you begin with the **Warm-up** questions in the right-hand column. There are usually three of these. The first is just an icebreaker to get the group talking to each other. It may or may not have anything to do with the topic. The second and third warm-up questions should take the group into the topic of the meeting.

After the warm-up questions, have group members take turns reading the **introductory comments** in the left-hand column. The comments are meant to introduce the topic and the Bible study on side two. Feel free to groan out loud (or applaud) while this section is read.

On side two you'll find a **Scripture passage** and six related **questions.** Before reading Scripture, take a look at question 1—it gives you something to look for while reading. Questions 1-3 help you get at important facts in the passage. Questions 4-6 help you interpret and apply the passage. Question 6 is especially important because it usually asks you to put some part of the Bible study into practice.

The **Group Talk** questions at the end raise some important real-life issues related to the topic. The questions help you exchange ideas for solving problems, based on your own day-to-day experiences.

That's it. I hope these studies help you grow closer to God and to each other.

In Christ,
Keith ("Flash") Stulp

The Crest Thing
(Start-up Meeting)

- Everybody in the group must introduce themselves by saying, "Hi! My name is _____ and my favorite toothpaste is _____." Also include the number of times (a) you tell the dental hygienist you floss; and (b) how many times you actually floss.

- In days of old, when knights and knightesses were bold, and they wore long woolly underwear to keep from getting cold, and they went to Ye Ol' Shoe Carnival to get their boots resoled, they rode around with crests on their shields (and you thought crest was a toothpaste). Notice the bees buzzing on the crest of our hero (at the right). The bees, of course, stand for truth. And naturally the solid bar between the bees stands for justice. Or something like that.

- Your turn now to do the crest thing. Use the shabby illustration on the back of this page and put the stuff on your crest that's listed there. When you're done, you get to explain your crest to the rest of the group.

- Talk about any prayer concerns or praise/thanks items you might have. Share these with the group and pray together. Hand-holding is acceptable.

ON THE CREST, DRAW

- your favorite cartoon character.

- a picture of your job or a job you wouldn't mind doing.

- a symbol of a hobby or something else you really enjoy.

- your family in stick figures.

- anything else you want to tell others about yourself.

DECISIONS

God Is in Control

Decisions, decisions, decisions. We spend every waking moment of our days making decisions. *Do I turn off my alarm and sleep or do I get up for school? Do I eat a plain bagel or raisin bagel? Do I want to sit in the driver's seat or steer from the passenger side?* When you think about it, we make decisions while we sleep too. *Do I run from the green monster with oozing tentacles or do I fight?*

Of course, many decisions are much more difficult to make. *Should I go to college or get a job? Which college should I go to? How can I convince the parental units that I need to borrow the car? Should I ask so-and-so out or decide that being alone is really a lot more fun?* Decisions can be gut-wrenching, time-consuming deals.

During the next five meetings, we'll look at decision-making and how we as Christians should approach it. For now, just remember one thing: God is in control. God is in the driver's seat. God decides where we're going and what route we'll take to get there. No matter what happens because of our decisions, we know we have a loving God on our side. That's good to know when we make decisions. That can give us peace.

1. When on an escalator, how do you get off?
   ___ Hold on to the hand rails and lift feet off the ground (gymnastic)
   ___ Sit on handrail (picturesque)
   ___ Jump over last step (athletic)
   ___ Leave feet on step and scrape off (gravitationally challenged)
   ___ Close eyes (daredevil)
   ___ Step backward for a couple of steps, then glide forward (dancer)
   ___ Other:

2. Rate yourself on "tough decisions I would make regarding my siblings."
   ___ Donate internal organ for sister or brother (hero)
   ___ Allow sibling to borrow the car on a weekend night (noble)
   ___ Do chore for sister or brother (humane)
   ___ Turn in sister or brother for borrowing clothes (inhumane)
   ___ Take early-morning pictures of sibling and give to yearbook staff (friend of Saddam Hussein)

3. Jesus made a very difficult decision in the garden of Gethsemane. What did he decide to do?

Isaiah 40:28-31

1. As you read this, notice what God does.

2. What are some of the great things God does for people?

3. What are some of the good images that show what will happen when we hope in God?

28 Do you not know?
    Have you not heard?
The LORD is the everlasting God,
    the Creator of the ends of the earth.
He will not grow tired or weary,
    and his understanding no one can fathom.
29 He gives strength to the weary
    and increases the power of the weak.
30 Even youths grow tired and weary,
    and young men stumble and fall;
31 but those who hope in the LORD
    will renew their strength.
They will soar on wings like eagles,
    they will run and not grow weary,
    they will walk and not be faint.

4. Why does the writer seem surprised at the beginning of this passage? Should we be surprised God is like this?

5. Pick a picture from verse 31 and tell what it might mean for your life:

___to soar (wake up bright and early? smile at breakfast? praise God for something good?)
___to run and not get tired (your ideas)
___to walk forever (your ideas)

6. What will you try to practice from this passage?

Group Talk

1. What sometimes stops us from making the right decisions?
2. Give an example of how God is capable of making our bad decisions right.
3. As a decision-maker, how would you like to change?

Choosing Wisely

What do you think—does God really care if we decide to have toast for breakfast instead of Cheerios, or if we decide to take a different route to school than we normally do, or if we decide to order a Quarter Pounder instead of a Big Mac? Does God offer any guidance in making such ordinary decisions?

There are, of course, all kinds of areas where God does more than offer guidance. In these areas God flat-out tells us what we need to decide. "Always tell the truth," God says. "Respect your parents." "Don't waste the good things I give you." "Don't mess with pornography or abuse your body with drugs." And so on. In these areas and many more, what God wants is as plain as the nose on your face. We still need to make decisions about these things, but if we follow God's plan for our lives, we really have no choice.

In other areas, God doesn't step in and tell us to do this or do that. Instead, God leaves these matters up to us to decide. Some are really trivial—for instance, deciding between a Quarter Pounder or a Big Mac (though what either might do to our arteries is a matter of debate). Some are much more significant: *Should I take the part-time job or try out for the play? Which college should I choose?* Some are real gut-wrenchers: *Should I tell my youth pastor about a friend's drug habit?* God doesn't clearly say do this or do that on decisions like these.

But in all our decisions, big and small, God does want us to decide wisely. Choosing wisely means living by the principles God gives us. Principles like stewardship (how we spend our money and time) or modesty (how we dress or act) need to be considered in the choices we make.

1. Check ear lobes. Those with attached lobes sit on one side of the circle; those with dangling lobes sit on the other.

2. What was a truly dumb decision you once made?
   ___ Picked up rope—turned out to be a snake.
   ___ Petted dog that "never bites."
   ___ Threw aerosol can in fire.
   ___ Took "shortcut" on hike.
   ___ Thought your parents wouldn't wait up for you.
   ___ Other:

3. For what kind of decisions do you usually ask God's help?

James 3:13-18

1. As you read this passage, think about what our deeds show about us.

2. Share an example of what you consider to be "selfish ambition" or "bitter envy."

3. What is supposed to take the place of selfish ambition and bitter envy, according to James?

[13]Who is wise and understanding among you? Let him show it by his good life, by deeds done in the humility that comes from wisdom. [14]But if you harbor bitter envy and selfish ambition in your hearts, do not boast about it or deny the truth. [15]Such "wisdom" does not come down from heaven but is earthly, unspiritual, of the devil. [16]For where you have envy and selfish ambition, there you find disorder and every evil practice.

[17]But the wisdom that comes from heaven is first of all pure; then peace-loving, considerate, submissive, full of mercy and good fruit, impartial and sincere. [18]Peacemakers who sow in peace raise a harvest of righteousness.

4. Look at the list in verse 17 that describes wisdom. Which of these qualities says something to you today? Which one would you like to have play a bigger role in your own decision-making?

5. What are the results of making wise decisions?

6. What will you take with you from this passage?

Group Talk

1. What would you rank as the "top three" big decisions in most people's lives?
2. Are there any decisions we make that don't affect others? If so, give some examples.
3. Think of a decision that you made recently that you feel good about, that seems like a wise decision. What motivated you to make that decision?

3 DECISIONS

START HERE →

*warm*UP

Tug-of-War

Last time we talked about decisions we needed to make without specific directions from God. In such decisions, we can only follow general principles God has laid out for us. We also mentioned other decisions that involve things God clearly forbids (gossiping, stealing, doing drugs—you know the rest). Of course, just because we know how to decide in situations involving these things doesn't always mean these are easy decisions to make. Knowing what to do and what is right doesn't mean we automatically do it.

Why don't we? Well, for one thing, sin can be very exciting. Fun too! Just because we know it is wrong doesn't mean we aren't attracted to it. And sometimes we make the wrong decision simply because our friends are making the same wrong decision, and we want them to accept us.

Like Paul in our passage for today, we sometimes feel we're right in the middle of a tug-of-war. We're pulled one way by what we know is right and another way by what we really want to do. Sometimes it can get so bad we feel we're going to literally come apart!

Fortunately, God doesn't leave us stranded in this mess. When we're so confused we don't know which end is up, we can find help. We can pray to the One who is in control. We can look for guiding principles in his Word. And we can bring our problem to people we regard as good sources of Christian wisdom: a close friend, a youth pastor, a parent, a teacher, or someone else whom we trust.

With God on our side, and with the help of his Word and the people he's placed in our lives, guess who's going to win the tug-of-war?

1. Given a choice, do you prefer
   ___ vanilla or chocolate?
   ___ sitting in back or in front?
   ___ thick crust or thin crust pizza?
   ___ windows down or air on (in car)?
   ___ dogs or cats?
   ___ stairs or escalator/elevator?
   ___ talk or silence in elevator?
   ___ comedy or drama?
   ___ summer or winter?

2. If I need help with a tough decision, I might talk to
   ___ my dog or cat.
   ___ the wall.
   ___ Mom or Dad.
   ___ Grandpa or Grandma.
   ___ a close friend.
   ___ a teacher.
   ___ my youth pastor or pastor.
   ___ God.
   ___ other:

Romans 7:15-24
(The Message)

What I don't understand about myself is that I decide one way, but then I act another, doing things I absolutely despise. So if I can't be trusted to figure out what is best for myself and then do it, it becomes obvious that God's command is necessary.

But I need something *more!* For if I know the law but still can't keep it, and if the power of sin within me keeps sabotaging my best intentions, I obviously need help! I realize that I don't have what it takes. I can will it, but I can't *do* it. I decide to do good, but I don't *really* do it; I decide not to do bad, but then I do it anyway. My decisions, such as they are, don't result in actions. Something has gone wrong deep within me and gets the better of me every time.

It happens so regularly that it's predictable. The moment I decide to do good, sin is there to trip me up. I truly delight in God's commands, but it's pretty obvious that not all of me joins in that delight. Parts of me covertly rebel, and just when I least expect it, they take charge.

I've tried everything and nothing helps. I'm at the end of my rope. Is there no one who can do anything for me?

1. As you read this passage, watch for the tug-of-war the author of this passage (Paul) is experiencing. Have you ever felt this way?

2. How does doing something "you absolutely despise" make you feel?

3. According to Paul, why do we do wrong when we know better? Does his answer make sense?

4. What does it mean to "delight" in God's commands? Do we actually do that?

5. How would you answer Paul's question at the end of this passage? Check out Romans 7:25 in your Bible to find Paul's own answer.

6. What will you try to do as a result of this Bible study? (How are you doing in trying to "live out" these passages?)

group Talk

1. What are some of the temptations you see people struggling with?
2. Give each other feedback on how to deal with these problems.

4 DECISIONS

warm UP

Not Just Me

Let's say you decide to use the money you saved from your part-time job at the Burger House to buy a brand-new, state-of-the-art computer. *It's my money*, you think. *I really need it for my work at school (OK, for the games too). Besides, it's my decision. No one else is affected but me, right?*

It's true that we usually think first about how our decisions affect our own lives. This is fairly normal, since we think about ourselves much more than we think of anyone else.

However, our decisions rarely affect only ourselves. Take that decision to buy the computer, for instance. Seems that you like it so much, your family sees you only for meals. And your kid brother keeps bugging you to let him use it. And you keep bugging your parents to spring for hooking up to the Net. And a couple of your friends are really eager to get their hands on your machine.

You made the decision to buy the computer for yourself. It sounded like it would affect only you. But lots of decisions we make about ourselves indirectly affect others. And, of course, many of our decisions directly involve others (you decide to share your computer with two friends). In both types of decisions, unwise choices generally bring about more unwise choices (to cover up the first mistake, etc.), and wise choices often bring about more wise decisions. So it's important to ask, "How will my decision affect others?"

You probably know the saying, "Jesus first, others second, myself last." It is generally a good piece of advice. Still, though we are last, we are created in God's image. We are God's children. We are far from insignificant! So it's wise to think about the impact of our choices on *ourselves*. But we also need to ask, "How will my decision affect those around me?" If the answer is "like an incoming Scud missile," it's back to the drawing board for sure!

1. What's one of the nicest Christmas presents you've ever received? Ever given?

2. When have you made a decision that went against the wishes of those around you (like your parents or your friends)? What happened? Did it prove to be the right decision in the end?

Acts 21:10-15
(The Message)

After several days of visiting, a prophet from Judea by the name of Agabus came down to see us. He went right up to Paul, took Paul's belt, and, in a dramatic gesture, tied himself up, hands and feet. He said, "This is what the Holy Spirit says: The Jews in Jerusalem are going to tie up the man who owns this belt just like this and hand him over to godless unbelievers."

When we heard that, we and everyone there that day begged Paul not to be stubborn and persist in going to Jerusalem. But Paul wouldn't budge: "Why all this hysteria? Why do you insist on making a scene and making it even harder for me? You're looking at this backwards. The issue in Jerusalem is not what they do to me, whether arrest or murder, but what the Master Jesus does through my obedience. Can't you see that?"

We saw that we weren't making even a dent in his resolve, and gave up. "It's in God's hands now," we said. "Master, you handle it."

It wasn't long before we had our luggage together and were on our way to Jerusalem.

1. As you read this, place yourself among Paul's friends. How would you have reacted to his plan to go to Jerusalem?

2. What guided Paul in making his decision not to listen to his friends? Did he show any concern for others?

3. What guided Paul's friends in making their decisions about Paul?

4. What do you think of Paul's decision?

___courageous
___stupid
___considerate of others
___ inconsiderate of others
___godly
___other:

5. What final decision do Paul's friends reach about his plans? What does this decision show about them?

6. What did you learn from this passage that could affect your decision-making during the week ahead?

group Talk

1. Why is it hard for us to serve others' needs before our own?
2. Tell about a time when you had to make a decision and found the advice of others helpful.
3. After making a decision, do you feel peace that it is in God's hands?

START HERE ➔

warm **UP**

1. What's the scariest movie you've seen?

2. Tell about a time when you were *really* scared.

3. What would you expect Jesus to say to you when you're afraid or anxious?

What! Me Worry?

What does a person get scared of? Some may fear coming to a new school. Some may fear failure—doing poorly in a certain class, not making the track team, getting turned down for a date. Still others may fear what's happening in their families—their parents aren't getting along or a family member is dealing with a serious illness. Did you know that the greatest fear of the average American is making public speeches? People are actually more afraid of public speaking than they are of death.

When we're afraid or anxious, someone invariably will say, "Hey! Don't worry!" Trouble is, it's not easy to just stop worrying when there seems to be so much to worry about. Few people live without some worries or fears. Just about everyone, for example, fears being rejected or being caught in some totally embarrassing situation.

Of course, a little fear can be a good thing. Fear of being run over by a cement truck keeps us from taking a nap on the highway. Fear keeps us on our toes when danger occurs. Fear can even give us positive energy to focus on some tasks (like public speaking, for instance).

While fear can be a natural and normal reaction in some situations, God doesn't want us living in a state of anxiety about what might happen in the future. Living in terror of what may happen shows a lack of trust in a God who is willing and able to take care of us. This is not to say we may not be *concerned* about a situation. While worry and fear stop us from acting, genuine concern motivates us to take steps to correct the situation.

It's important to face our fears and anxieties. Begin by pinning down exactly what makes you afraid or anxious. Then talk to God about it. It can also be helpful to talk to someone you trust about your problem. Develop some sort of plan for dealing with the fear when it returns to trouble you.

Decreasing our fears and anxieties and relying more on God should be a goal of our Christian lives. As Jehoshaphat said to God when the chips were completely down against him and the rest of Judah: "We do not know what to do, but our eyes are upon you" (2 Chron. 20:12).

Matthew 6:25-34

1. As you read this, look for reasons why worrying doesn't help. Review them with the group.

2. When Jesus advises us not to worry about our life, he means that

___everything's coming up roses from now on.
___God always bails us out of every troublesome situation.
___in the long run God will work everything out for our good.
___other:

3. "But seek first his kingdom . . . and all these things will be given to you as well" means

___sell your car and bike everywhere.
___put God first and he'll put you in a new Mercedes.
___put God first and he'll take care of your needs.
___put God first and hang on to your car and everything else.
___other:

[25]Therefore, I tell you, do not worry about your life, what you will eat or drink; or about your body, what you will wear. Is not life more important than food, and the body more important than clothes? [26]Look at the birds of the air; they do not sow or reap or store away in barns, and yet your heavenly father feeds them. Are you not much more valuable than they? [27]Who of you by worrying can add a single hour to his life?

[28]And why do you worry about clothes? See how the lilies of the field grow. They do not labor or spin. [29]Yet I tell you that not even Solomon in all his splendor was dressed like one of these. [30]If that is how God clothes the grass of the field, which is here today and tomorrow is thrown into the fire, will he not much more clothe you, O you of little faith? [31]So do not worry, saying, "What shall we eat?" or "What shall we drink?" or "What shall we wear?" [32]For the pagans run after all these things, and your heavenly Father knows that you need them. [33]But seek first his kingdom and his righteousness, and all these things will be given to you as well. [34]Therefore, do not worry about tomorrow, for tomorrow will worry about itself. Each day has enough trouble of its own.

4. Jesus says tomorrow will take care of itself. Does that rule out making plans or being concerned? Why or why not? What responsibilities do we have for "tomorrow"?

5. Jesus says not to worry about food or drink or clothing. What do you think he would add to his list if he were visiting your high school today?

6. Pick a phrase from today's Scripture that you will carry with you throughout the week, something you can say to yourself when the fears hit and the worries come. Share your phrase with the group.

group Talk

1. Mom says, "Come in by midnight or I'll worry." Do you quote her the above passage and tell her to stop sinning? Good idea?
2. Share with the group an event or situation that's causing fear/anxiety in your life. Give/receive feedback as to how this problem could be handled.

FEAR

No Fear

Last week, we noted the difference between being worried and being concerned. Worry stops us from action, and concern motivates us to act. This meeting will focus on Jesus and how he dealt with the pain and terror of the cross when he was in Gethsemane.

It's impossible to fully understand what Jesus faced in Gethsemane. On the one hand, he knew what was ahead: that he would rise again from the dead and that all would be well. On the other hand, he must have dreaded the beating and crucifixion that was coming. Even more frightening must have been the idea of being totally separated from God, suffering the pangs of hell itself. Facing this must have been terrifying.

So what did Jesus do? First, he surrounded himself with his best friends. They turned out to be of little comfort, but Jesus still wanted their moral support. Jesus also took time by himself to pray—hard. He pleaded with his Father to skip the whole deal. But he ended by saying, "Not what I want but what you want." He trusted in the Father to work it all out.

And that's our great hope in life as well. No matter what happens, God is in control. God will work things out. Our lifeline is the promise: "Never will I leave you; never will I forsake you" (Heb. 13:5).

1. Before some big event that you have a key part in, do you
   ___ want to hurl?
   ___ get huge butterflies?
   ___ say "What! Me worry?"
   ___ cry to Mommy?
   ___ pace around the room?
   ___ comb the dog?
   ___ pray?
   ___ yawn?
   ___ other:

2. What kind of situations give you butterflies?

3. What do you think—was Jesus ever afraid?

Matthew 26:36-46
(The Message)

1. As you read this, put yourself in the disciples' shoes. What would you likely have done?

2. How would you describe Jesus' feelings in Gethsemane?

3. When Jesus prays, "Do it your way," what does he mean? What do you mean when you pray for God's will to be done?

Then Jesus went with them to a garden called Gethsemane and told his disciples, "Stay here while I go over there and pray." Taking along Peter and the two sons of Zebedee, he plunged into an agonizing sorrow. Then he said, "This sorrow is crushing my life out. Stay here and keep vigil with me."

Going a little ahead, he fell on his face, praying, "My Father, if there is any way, get me out of this. But please, not what I want. You, what do *you* want?"

When he came back to his disciples, he found them sound asleep. He said to Peter, "Can't you stick it out with me a single hour? Stay alert; be in prayer so you don't wander into temptation without even knowing you're in danger. There is a part of you that is eager, ready for anything in God. But there's another part that's as lazy as an old dog sleeping by the fire."

He then left them a second time. Again he prayed, "My Father, if there is no other way than this, drinking this cup to the dregs, I'm ready. Do it your way."

When he came back, he again found them sound asleep. They simply couldn't keep their eyes open. This time he let them sleep on, going over the same ground one last time.

When he came back the next time, he said, "Are you going to sleep on and make a night of it? My time is up, the Son of Man is about to be handed over to the hands of sinners. Get up! Let's get going! My betrayer is here."

4. In what way is Jesus a model for us when we face fears and anxieties? You may want to recall how Jesus acted when the mob came to get him (Matt. 26:47ff.).

5. Share with the group a time when it was hard for you to say "Your will be done" to God.

6. What will you take with you from this passage and today's discussion?

group Talk

1. When you're worried or scared about something, what helps you deal with it?
2. What can we do to help others work through their fears and anxieties?

GOSSIP

It Hurts

- "Did you hear about the party at Mark's house last night? His parents came home early and beer bottles were all over the place."

- "Dave says Corrie got hauled out of English class and had to go to the office—Dave thinks it might have to do with her skipping school three days last week."

- "I'm not supposed to repeat this, but if you promise not to tell *anyone,* yesterday Janelle told me that . . . "

It's almost impossible to spend a day in high school without hearing some juicy gossip or rumor. It's incredible how rapidly a hot rumor can make its way through the whole school. A whispered conversation at a locker, a note, a chat over lunch . . . and rumors fly. Not that high schools are the only places where people gossip, of course. It happens everywhere—in homes, on the job, even at church. And wherever it happens, it hurts if you're the one being talked about.

There's a difference, of course, between simply passing along information and gossiping. For example, to say, "Steve is in the hospital" would usually not be gossiping (unless, of course, this was only hearsay or was private information that Steve and his family did not want to be made public). But to say, "Steve is in the hospital. I hear it's from a drug overdose!" comes much closer to gossip.

Gossip is the act of spreading rumors about someone else that are not true or not known to be true. Talking about who is sleeping with whom and who got drunk at such and such a party is gossip. Gossip can also be the spread of true information of a personal or private nature that was never meant to be shared. Gossip tears down the reputation of others while building up the reputation of the one spreading the gossip.

That's one reason why we continue to gossip—it makes us look good. Compared to what "so and so" is doing, we're as pure as fresh snow! And when we have a juicy story to tell about someone, we can be the center of attention—for a while at least.

Gossiping hurts others. It really shouldn't be done by people who claim to follow their Lord's command to treat others with love and respect.

1. OK, imagine that you're camping in some remote wilderness. What would be worse: waking up to find a snake on your pillow or waking up to see a bear poking his nose into your tent?

2. Rumors are almost as unwanted as snakes on your pillow and bears in your tent. They can also be frightening and harmful. Without getting into names, mention a rumor that you've recently heard. How did it get started? Was it harmless or harmful?

3. Why do you think God hates gossip?

selections from proverbs

A gossip betrays a confidence, but a trustworthy man keeps a secret (11:13).

There are six things the LORD hates, seven that are detestable to him: haughty eyes, a lying tongue, hands that shed innocent blood, a heart that devises wicked schemes, feet that are quick to rush into evil, a false witness who pours out lies, and a man who stirs up dissension among brothers (6:16-19).

Reckless words pierce like a sword, but the tongue of the wise brings healing. Truthful lips endure forever, but a lying tongue lasts only a moment (12:18-19).

. . . a gossip separates close friends (16:28).

Without wood a fire goes out; without gossip a quarrel dies down (26:20).

Like a club or a sword or a sharp arrow is the man who gives false testimony against his neighbor (25:18).

The words of a gossip are like choice morsels; they go down to a man's inmost parts (18:8).

He who guards his mouth and his tongue keeps himself from calamity (21:23).

A lying tongue hates those it hurts, and a flattering mouth works ruin (26:28).

Titus 3:1-2

Remind the people to . . . be ready to do whatever is good, to slander no one, to be peaceable and considerate, and to show true humility toward all men.

1. As you read, notice how gossip affects those whom it contacts.

2. According to Proverbs 25:18, what is a gossip like?

3. What are the effects of telling the truth and controlling what you say?

4. Do you gossip sometimes? If so, why? Do you feel the need to be reminded of the good stuff in Titus 3? Why or why not?

5. Instead of relating negatively to others through gossip, how can we be positive towards those around us?

6. What will you try to do differently this week as a result of today's discussion?

group Talk

1. How does gossip hurt the person doing the gossiping (as well as the person being discussed)?
2. Talk to each other about learning how to speak truthfully and resist gossip. What has helped you? Might it help, for example, to think of yourself stabbing someone every time you say something bad about him or her?
3. Is reading the *National Enquirer* and similar magazines a bad thing to do? Why do those magazines appeal to people?

START HERE →

How Jesus Handled It

Imagine a place where you could be yourself, and yet never need to worry about what people would say about you behind your back or to your face. If you said or did something stupid, no one would kid you or mock you about it.

You don't really need to imagine this place. It's real. It's called heaven, otherwise known as the new earth (see Rev. 20). Heaven will be lots of great and incredible things, far better than we can begin to imagine. But one very nice thing about it will be the total lack of gossip. No more rumor-spreading, no more unkind words, no more hatred.

As children of God, we've got all that and much more to look forward to. Someday. But get this—the kingdom of God is not only coming "someday," it's already here. Jesus has come, the enemy is on the run, and the Spirit is working in our lives to make us more and more like Jesus every day.

Keeping all that in mind gives us good motivation to start practicing here what we'll someday enjoy in the new earth. One important part of that is how we use God's gift of speech. So instead of spreading gossip and tearing each other down, we ought to be building each other up.

Why do people gossip? It's an easy way to appear important. It builds us up while it tears others down. When we gossip, we appear to be better than the people we are gossiping about.

Jesus would have none of this. Those who met him were touched by how much he cared about everyone, and he shared himself with them as well. Today we'll look at how Jesus treated a woman who had gone through five husbands and was no doubt the number one target of gossip for miles around. Our story begins when Jesus and his disciples, hot and tired from traveling, came to a well in the Samaritan town of Sychar . . .

1. OK, what would be better: inheriting a million bucks or having lifetime free air travel, hotel, restaurant meals, and the car of your choice?

2. What do you think heaven (the new earth) will be like?
   ___ like church, only it lasts forever
   ___ complete freedom to do exactly as I please
   ___ living in a mansion on a street paved with pure gold
   ___ living in the presence of Jesus
   ___ flying around with the angels
   ___ lots of harp music and singing
   ___ a place to laugh and laugh
   ___ like the earth today, only without the bad stuff
   ___ exciting—new bods for everyone!
   ___ a place to see people I love who have died
   ___ something better than I can ever imagine
   ___ other:

Excerpts from John 4:7-30
(The Message)

A woman, a Samaritan, came to draw water. Jesus said, "Would you give me a drink of water?" (His disciples had gone to the village to buy food for lunch.)

The Samaritan woman, taken aback, asked, "How come you, a Jew, are asking me, a Samaritan woman, for a drink?" (Jews in those days wouldn't be caught dead talking to Samaritans).

Jesus answered, "If you knew the generosity of God and who I am, you would be asking *me* for a drink, and I would give you fresh, living water . . . Everyone who drinks this water will get thirsty again and again. Anyone who drinks the water I give will never thirst—not ever." . . .

The woman said, "Sir, give me this water so I won't ever get thirsty, won't ever have to come back to this well again!"

He said, "Go call your husband and then come back."

"I have no husband," she said.

". . . You've had five husbands and the man you're living with now isn't even your husband."

"Oh, so you're a prophet! Well, tell me this: Our ancestors worshiped God at this mountain, but you Jews insist that Jerusalem is the only place for worship, right?"

"Believe me, woman, the time is coming when you Samaritans will worship the Father neither here at this mountain nor there in Jerusalem. . . . It's who you are and the way you live that count before God. . . . Those who worship him must do it out of their very being . . ."

The woman said, "I don't know about that. I do know that the Messiah is coming. When he arrives, we'll get the whole story."

"I am he," said Jesus. "You don't have to wait any longer or look any further."

Just then his disciples came back. They were shocked. They couldn't believe he was talking with that kind of a woman. . . .

The woman took the hint and left. . . . Back in the village she told the people, "Come see a man who knew all about the things I did. . . . Do you think this could be the Messiah?" And they went out to see for themselves.

1. As you read this story, look for the "dirt" that Jesus had on the Samaritan woman.

2. What does Jesus do with it?

___lets it color his feelings before he even talks to the woman
___eagerly shares it with the disciples
___uses it to put down the woman every chance he gets
___uses it to confront her in a caring way
___other:

3. Why are the disciples shocked by all this? Can you understand their reaction? Would we have reacted in the same way?

4. What is the woman's response when she realizes that Jesus knows all about her?

___anger
___defensiveness
___fear
___disbelief
___relief
___other:

5. How do we tend to react when people know secrets about us?

6. What can you learn from Jesus' example that you intend to practice this week?

Group Talk

1. The woman was vulnerable with Jesus (whether she wanted to be or not). In response, what did Jesus tell her that he had not yet told anyone about himself? What does the fact that Jesus told this to a Samaritan woman who had five husbands tell you about him?

2. Why is it hard to share stuff about ourselves even with our friends (when Jesus could be vulnerable with complete strangers)? Do you think such sharing is important?

How We Can Handle It

You've probably heard the old saying "Sticks and stones may break my bones, but names will never hurt me." Really? It doesn't hurt to be called a nerd or a brain or retarded or porky or toothpick or pizza-face? It doesn't hurt to be on the receiving end of a crude racial put-down? It doesn't hurt to be whispered about and laughed at? Maybe people just say names don't hurt them as a kind of defense against something that hurts a great deal.

Words have tremendous power—to hurt but also to heal and to help. With some care and effort, we can break the habit of using words to hurt; we can replace that habit with good words, words that encourage, words that affirm and build up. If some words are not positive, even if they are factual, consider not saying them. Always question your motives when talking about others.

Suppose that someone you know is truly deserving of being called a jerk. Suppose someone has gotten himself or herself into a genuine mess. May you talk about that person with your friends? How do you know when a comment is appropriate or when it is simply gossip? Here are some good questions to ask yourself before commenting about another person: Would I say this in front of that person? Would I call him a jerk if he were standing right there? Would I spread that story about her if she were listening?

Every person on earth has hurt others with his or her words. Every person struggles to control what comes out of his or her mouth. "No person can tame the tongue. It is a restless evil, full of deadly poison" (James 3:7). We need help, God's help. Ask for it! And use the grace and power the Holy Spirit gives you to speak words that heal instead of hurt. Continue to bring the kingdom of heaven to earth with your words.

1. OK, last time. What's worse: forgetting that you have this huge English test next hour or having a teacher overhear you imitating his or her peculiar way of talking?

2. Sometimes the negative words we use to describe others can be replaced by more positive ones. What would you rather be called?

weird	or	unique
talkative	or	friendly
brainy	or	bright
nosy	or	inquisitive

   Come up with a few of your own!

3. Can you picture yourself passing along some choice bit of gossip to God when you're praying? (Just for thinking about.)

Psalm 57:4-11
(The Message)

A psalm of David, who had a rough go of it for much of his life.

I find myself in a pride of lions
    who are wild for a taste of human flesh;
their teeth are lances and arrows,
    their tongues are sharp daggers.
Soar high over the skies, O God!
    Cover the whole earth with your glory!

They booby-trapped my path;
    I thought I was dead and done for.
They dug a mantrap to catch me,
    and fell in headlong themselves.

I'm ready, God, so ready,
    ready to sing from head to toe,
Ready to sing, ready to raise a tune:
    "Wake up, soul!
Wake up, harp! Wake up, lute!
    Wake up, you sleepyhead sun!"

I'm thanking you, God, out loud in the streets,
    singing your praises in town and country.
The deeper your love, the higher it goes;
    every cloud is a flag to your faithfulness.

Soar high in the skies, O God!
    Cover the whole earth with your glory!

1. It's thought that David wrote this psalm while hiding in a cave from King Saul and his men, who were trying to kill him. As you read this, watch for lines that give you a good idea of how fierce his enemies were. Check the line that shows his enemies were also attempting to hurt him with rumors and lies.

2. Picture David hiding in the cave at night, surrounded by his enemies. How does he manage to cope and to get beyond his fear? What does he focus on?

3. What do you think of the ways that David will praise God when God saves him from his enemies? If you wanted to praise God for getting you out of a mess, what would you do?

4. Sometimes we are "attacked" by words that make us feel like "hiding in a cave." Mention a situation from your experience that made you feel that way.

5. When you're hurting from the sting of someone's words, what helps you? What in David's psalm suggests how we might be helped in these times?

6. Take turns or have someone in your group read Psalm 57 as your group's expression of praise to God.

group Talk

1. If you hear gossip about someone you know, what should you do?
2. If you learn that people have been spreading gossip about you, what should you do?
3. "What you see is what you look for." Is this true, and how does this apply to gossip?

The Future

In this group of Bible studies, we'll look at several things that can drive us up the wall, things that make us feel stressed out and done in. The future, with all its uncertainties, can be one of those things. Worrying about tomorrow's test or date, about getting a summer job, about going to college, about deciding on a career . . . all of these can really stress us out. Any change, for better or for worse, can be scary.

But doing the same old same old has its pitfalls as well. In his book *God Came Near,* Max Lucado talks about one of Satan's favorite companions: familiarity. Familiarity lulls us to sleep. It makes us feel secure. We forget what is important.

The Unknown is a different breed. It makes us nervous. It makes us wish for same old same old. It also makes us want to rely more on God. And isn't that the point? Anne Shirley, of *Anne of Green Gables* fame, has the right idea about the future. She says that at one time the future stretched out before her like a straight road. Now, however, a bend appears in the road. "I don't know what lies around the bend. But I'm going to believe the best does. It has a fascination all its own, that bend. . . . I wonder how the road beyond it goes—what there is of green glory and soft checked light and shadows—what new landscapes—what new beauties—what curves and hills and valleys further on."

Jesus understands our apprehension about what is to come. He knows what it feels like to face the future alone. Just before he left his disciples to return to heaven, he said, "I am with you always, to the very end of the age" (Matt. 28:20). No matter what bend we see in the road ahead, we won't be traveling that road alone.

In our Bible passage for today, God appears to Moses in a burning bush, then shakes up his future by giving him a "mission impossible." Check it out on page 36.

1. It's stress time—only in your dreams. Share a dream (or more likely a nightmare) that makes you really want to wake up quickly (for example, you're late for class and you're running around the halls looking for your locker).

2. Describe one experience you've had of being absolutely new to something (new school, new neighborhood, new church—you get the idea). What was the worst part of it?

3. If you were God, how would you get "your people" to turn more toward you?

Excerpts from Exodus 3

[7]The LORD said, "I have indeed seen the misery of my people in Egypt. . . . [8]So I have come down to rescue them from the hand of the Egyptians and to bring them out of that land into a good and spacious land. . . ." [10]So now, go. I am sending you to Pharaoh to bring my people the Israelites out of Egypt.

[11]But Moses said to God, "Who am I, that I should go to Pharaoh and bring the Israelites out of Egypt?"

[12]And God said, "I will be with you. And this will be the sign to you that it is I who have sent you: When you have brought the people out of Egypt, you will worship God on this mountain."

[13]Moses said to God, "Suppose I go to the Israelites and say to them, 'The God of your fathers has sent me to you,' and they ask me, 'What is his name?' Then what shall I tell them?"

[14]God said to Moses, "I AM WHO I AM. This is what you are to say to the Israelites. 'I AM' has sent me to you. . . . "

[16]"Go, assemble the elders of Israel and say to them, 'The LORD, the God of your fathers—the God of Abraham, Isaac, and Jacob—appeared to me and said: I have watched over you and have seen what has been done to you in Egypt. [17]And I have promised to bring you up out of your misery in Egypt into . . . a land flowing with milk and honey.

[18]"The elders of Israel will listen to you. Then you and the elders are to go to the king of Egypt and say to him, 'The LORD, the God of the Hebrews, has met with us. Let us take a three-day journey into the desert to offer sacrifices to the LORD our God.' [19]But I know that the king of Egypt will not let you go unless a mighty hand compels him. [20]So I will stretch out my hand and strike the Egyptians with all the wonders that I will perform among them. After that, he will let you go."

1. As you read this story, think how you would react if you were Moses.

2. God makes some awesome promises here. What are they? How does Moses react? How do you imagine him saying these things to God?

3. What assurances about the future did Moses have from God? What assurances do we have?

4. Do you ever feel like Moses did (Whoa! Wait a minute! You want me to do what?!) when you think about the future? If you wish, share some of your anxieties with the group.

5. What might stop you from really believing that God has control of the future?

___I'm not sure if I really trust God.
___God doesn't seem that concerned—too many bad things happen.
___I don't love God enough—I might be punished.
___Nothing, really. I honestly believe God is in control.
___Other:

6. What single thought from today's discussion will you try to take with you into the future (that's next hour and next year)?

Group Talk

1. Share with the group how you handle uncertainty about the future.
2. God says, "I know the plans I have for you. Plans to prosper you and not to harm you, plans to give you hope and a future. . . . You will seek me and find me when you seek me with all your heart" (Jer. 29:11, 13). Why doesn't everything always turn out great if this is true? Talk together how you handle disappointment with God and with the future that God controls.
3. Share your personal feelings about facing the future with God.

START HERE →

*warm*UP

Busyness

"This is insanity!" How often do we say that to ourselves when we think of how busy we are? There's school seven or eight hours a day—a huge time commitment that's equal to a full-time job. After school, there may be a part-time job at Joe's Burgers that gets you home after nine maybe two or three times a week. Or there may be cross-country practice or play practice or taking care of a younger brother or sister at home or debate team or the school newspaper or any of dozens of other activities. And don't forget studying for tomorrow's test and writing that paper for English. Oh, and there's a youth meeting at church tonight to discuss the next service project, and tomorrow morning before school is your once-a-week Bible study group . . . and so it goes. Life can be a real rat race.

In spite of our complaints, being busy can be good for us. Even God gives us lots to do: "Be fruitful and multiply . . . subdue the earth . . . make disciples of all nations . . . obey your parents . . . go to the ant, you sluggard . . . love one another . . . work out your salvation . . . six days do your work . . . " Whew! On top of that, God has some really negative things to say about idleness.

But how much is too much? Jesus himself was often terribly busy, working day and night to the point of exhaustion. He was followed everywhere by crowds looking for miracles. Sometimes he and the disciples didn't even have time to eat (sound familiar?). Yet even Jesus found time to pray alone and to lead his disciples away to rest.

Jesus' example is a good one to follow. Stay busy! Work hard! But take breaks. God calls us to take some time off (remember that the Creator of heaven and earth rested on the seventh day). And before you take on a new responsibility, ask yourself some questions: Is it necessary and helpful for me to do this? Will it get in the way of my most important relationships (with God, family, and others)? Work and other activities—even if for the best of causes—are harmful and unproductive in the long run if they keep you from these relationships and if they lead to personal exhaustion.

1. If you are driving your car at the speed of light and you turn the lights on, what will happen?

2. If you have time on your hands, do you
   ___ walk your gerbil?
   ___ help your mom bake?
   ___ read something just for fun (not for school assignment)?
   ___ watch a little TV?
   ___ help your little brother make a model airplane?
   ___ make nuclear bomb with your Acme chemistry kit?
   ___ hold up a fork in front of you and imagine everyone you see is in prison?
   ___ call Aunt Gladys and thank her for sending a birthday card with money in it?
   ___ fill the Froot Loops cereal box with Corn Flakes?
   ___ go running with your Walkman?
   ___ other:

3. How do you picture Jesus spending his time? How busy was he?

Genesis 2:2-3

[2]By the seventh day God had finished the work he had been doing; so on the seventh day he rested from all his work. [3]And God blessed the seventh day and made it holy, because on it he rested from all the work of creating that he had done.

2 Thessalonians 3:10

For even when we were with you, we gave you this rule: "If a man will not work, he shall not eat."

Mark 6:30-31

[30]The apostles gathered around Jesus and reported to him all they had done and taught. [31]Then, because so many people were coming and going that they did not even have a chance to eat, he said to them, "Come with me by yourselves to a quiet place and get some rest."

Matthew 14:22-23

[22]Immediately Jesus made the disciples get into the boat and go on ahead of him to the other side, while he dismissed the crowd. [23]After he had dismissed them, he went up on a mountainside by himself to pray. When evening came, he was there alone. . . .

1 Timothy 5:8

If anyone does not provide for his relatives, and especially for his immediate family, he has denied the faith and is worse than an unbeliever.

1. As you read these verses, listen for the balance between work and rest that sets the pattern for our lives.

2. Do you ever think of Jesus as being a very busy person? What do you see him and his disciples doing with their time?

3. What kinds of things do you think Jesus and the disciples did to take a break from all their busyness?

4. God sets a pattern of resting one day in seven. What does it mean to you to "rest" on Sunday? How is Sunday different from the other days of the week? (Remember that Christians can differ on this point!)

5. God doesn't want us to be so busy that we neglect our relationship with him and with our family (see 1 Tim. 5:8). In your own life, do you find yourself so busy that you neglect these things? How busy is too busy?

6. What work does God call you to do today? In what ways will you attempt to take a break from your work to have time for God and family?

Group Talk

1. Reflect on what is most important in your life (work, school, family, church, sports, rest, and so on). Discuss within the group the rationale for your choices.
2. What are the warning signs that we are too busy?
3. Discuss how we might change our lives so that we're less busy.

START HERE → *warm*UP

Self-Esteem

Last time we talked about how busyness can be a way of life for some of us and how it can hurt our relationships with God and with our families. But an important question to ask is, "Why do we keep ourselves so busy?" Because of the culture we live in and our own family backgrounds, most of us work very hard to be successful. But for what purpose?

When people succeed in sports or get good grades or land a major role in the school play, they are often viewed as "awesome." However, when they don't make the team or when they bomb on the test or are rejected for the play, they are often viewed (or view themselves) as failures. And when you get out of school, people will often ask what you do. They'll expect you to respond in terms of the job you hold. Seems our value is summed up in our achievements. If we don't do something impressive, we're thought of as failures.

But that's not what the Bible teaches. It says that God loves us and thinks highly of us. God doesn't love us conditionally. God doesn't love us less if we get a C+ instead of an A. And yet, so many people put themselves under enormous stress to be successful. If God accepts us and loves us without looking at our achievements, shouldn't we view ourselves and others the same way?

Not that we don't need to try our best. God expects that. But God never said we had to weave our self-worth into it all. In fact, knowing we are loved and accepted regardless of how things turn out gives us the freedom to try hard. Our task is simply to do our best.

Unfortunately, accepting people because they are important in spite of what they do or don't do is not standard practice in high school. What would happen in your school if you really worked at helping the kids around you feel accepted and liked? How might things change?

1. If someone asks, "Who are you?" how would you answer them without describing what you do? To get you started, check the "non-doing" items on the list below—that is, items that describe who you are, not what you do. Then jot down an additional "non-doing" item of your own that describes who you are.
   ___ I play basketball.
   ___ I'm a Christian.
   ___ I raise angleworms.
   ___ I'm honest.
   ___ I get A's.
   ___ I'm considerate.
   ___ I listen.
   ___ I can touch my nose with my tongue.

   Additional non-doing item that describes me:

2. Why do people find it easier to say something negative about others than something positive?

3. In the Beatitudes (Matt. 5:1-12) Jesus said, "Blessed are the _____." Fill in the blank as many times as you can.

proverbs 16:3

Commit to the LORD whatever you do, and your plans will succeed.

Luke 12:6-7

⁶Are not five sparrows sold for two pennies? Yet not one of them is forgotten by God. ⁷Indeed, the very hairs of your head are all numbered. Don't be afraid; you are worth more than many sparrows.

Luke 16:19-25

¹⁹"There was a rich man who was dressed in purple and fine linen and lived in luxury every day. ²⁰At his gate was laid a beggar named Lazarus, covered with sores ²¹and longing to eat what fell from the rich man's table. Even the dogs came and licked his sores.

²²"The time came when the beggar died and the angels carried him to Abraham's side. The rich man also died and was buried. ²³In hell, where he was in torment, he looked up and saw Abraham far away, with Lazarus by his side. ²⁴So he called to him, 'Father Abraham, have pity on me and send Lazarus to dip the tip of his finger in water and cool my tongue, because I am in agony in this fire.'

²⁵"But Abraham replied, 'Son, remember that in your lifetime you received your good things, while Lazarus received bad things, but now he is comforted here and you are in agony.'"

1. As you read these passages, ask yourself how they relate to your value as a person.

2. What do you think it means to "commit to the Lord whatever you do"? What does God promise if we do that?

3. Does the number of hairs on your head have to do with something you do or who you are (in God's eyes)?

4. By the world's standards, who appeared to be more successful, the rich man or Lazarus? In God's terms, who was the greater success? Why?

5. Who is "the rich man" and who is "Lazarus" in your life today? How will you try to look at them differently?

6. What will you remember and attempt to practice from our Bible study and discussion today?

group Talk

1. Do guys or girls have a harder time complimenting each other? Why?
2. What kind of compliments do you like to receive? What kind (if any) do you dislike?
3. What can we do that will help us view others for who they are, not just for their accomplishments?

4 STRESSORS

START HERE → *warm* **UP**

Expectations

Why is it that two people can live similar lives, get the same grades, play the same sports with the same ability, have the same group of friends, work at the same kinds of jobs, make the same amount of money (take a breath if you're reading this out loud), and yet one person can be very satisfied with his or her life and the other very unhappy? It comes down to one little word: expectations. OK, so it's not quite a little word; you get the idea.

Expectations—what we aspire to (or others want us to aspire to)—can be good. For example, if we expect to be good students, we might set the goal of getting nothing less than a B+ in any course. So we work hard not to let ourselves down. We've got something to shoot for, to work at. We've got a goal and a plan to reach it.

Other people's expectations of us can also be helpful. We may work extra hard because we don't want to let other people (like our parents) down. Because a coach says we can cut two minutes off our best cross-country time, we try like crazy to do just that. Because a teacher says he expects a really good paper from us, we do our best to deliver.

Naturally, expectations can have a downside. Continually wanting to be someone we are not is not only frustrating but also self-defeating. When we realize we can never look like her or play ball like him, we have a hard time being content with who we really are. And if other people set truly impossible standards for us (like never getting anything less than a 4.0 in high school), the pressure can turn us into a basket case.

So is it bad to have great expectations of yourself? Not at all. It's tremendously satisfying to strive to reach a difficult goal—and then finally get there. But remember this: we are not what we achieve, at least in God's sight. Our value to God depends entirely on our relationship to Jesus Christ, not on our own good deeds or accomplishments. If we love Jesus, God says to us: "You are my child, made in my image. I love you. I accept you. Come and learn from me what you can do and become."

Keep that perspective in mind the next time you're stressed out by somebody's great expectations.

1. If life truly is a thirst, what flavor is yours?

2. Mention one expectation you have for yourself.

3. What expectations do you think God has for you?

Deuteronomy 10:12-13

[12]And now, O Israel, what does the LORD your God ask of you but to fear the LORD your God, to walk in all his ways, to love him, to serve the LORD your God with all your heart and with all your soul, [13]and to observe the LORD's commands and decrees that I am giving you today for your own good?

Romans 8:1

There is now no condemnation for those who are in Christ Jesus. . . .

Ephesians 2:8-9

[8]For it is by grace you have been saved, through faith—and this not from yourselves, it is the gift of God—[9]not by works, so that no one can boast.

1. As you read this, listen for five things God expects of us.

2. Do these expectations seem like a lot or a little to you? On our own what kind of chance would we have of meeting them?

3. How do the passages from Romans 8 and Ephesians 2 "balance out" God's expectations in the Deuteronomy passage?

4. Do you honestly feel that in Christ you are accepted and loved by God, or do you feel burdened or maybe even crushed by God's expectations?

5. Ephesians 2:8-9 is really the heart of what we believe. Try turning these verses into a personal statement about what you believe about your salvation.

6. Pick a single thought from today's meeting that will help you deal with the stress of people (including yourself) expecting too much of you. Share that thought with others and try to remember it when you feel stressed.

Group Talk

1. To what extent are your own expectations or those of others stressors for you?
   __ a lot   __ not much   __ it depends
2. What are some of the consequences (positive and negative) when our expectations are higher than we can achieve?
3. What should we do if our expectations differ from those our parents have for us?

Spiritual Highs and Lows

Ever come back from a retreat or youth convention really feeling good about your relationship with Christ, full of praise for God, and wishing the experience could go on forever?

That's called a spiritual high. It's a time when we feel fired up about our relationship with God, a time when we might actually look forward to devotions and prayer. These "mountaintop" experiences can give our faith a tremendous boost. The downside is that our normal, day-to-day spiritual life suddenly looks kind of ordinary and dull. We want to stay close to God, keep our spiritual life in high gear. When we can't, we can feel guilty and stressed and disappointed.

When we feel that way, we need to face the facts: our relationship with God can't always be a mountaintop experience. A continuous spiritual high just isn't possible or even normal. Why not? Because all our relationships—including our relationship with God—have high points and low points, emotionally and otherwise. Furthermore, a deep relationship weathers storms; it handles times of doubt and questioning. So don't feel guilty if your faith flops back to earth after soaring. It happens all the time. It's "normal."

It's great to be on the mountaintop with God. But the life God calls us to is in the valleys. A fine Christian writer, Oswald Chambers, once said, "The height of the mountaintop is measured by the dismal drudgery of the valley, but it is in the valley that we have to live for the glory of God. We *see* his glory on the mount, but we never *live* for his glory there. It is in the place of humiliation that we find our true worth to God—that is where our faithfulness is revealed."

1. What are some natural "highs" for you?
   ___ getting an A on a big paper
   ___ the last day of school
   ___ having a date with the person of your dreams
   ___ running/jogging
   ___ lifting weights
   ___ walking (as in hiking maybe)
   ___ listening to favorite band/group
   ___ being kissed by your dog
   ___ other:

2. Where do you tend to experience your *spiritual* highs?

3. What qualities in Jesus make you want to have him as a friend?

Mark 9:2-10

1. As you read this, note where the action takes place.

2. What things must have made this an incredible spiritual high for the disciples? How do you think they felt coming back down the mountain?

3. Brainstorm some ideas about why Peter said what he did. What would you have said, and how would you have said it?

²After six days Jesus took Peter, James and John with him and led them up a high mountain, where they were all alone. There he was transfigured before them. ³His clothes became dazzling white, whiter than anyone in the world could bleach them. ⁴And there appeared before them Elijah and Moses, who were talking with Jesus.

⁵Peter said to Jesus, "Rabbi, it is good for us to be here. Let us put up three shelters—one for you, one for Moses and one for Elijah." ⁶(He did not know what to say, they were so frightened.)

⁷Then a cloud appeared and enveloped them, and a voice came from the cloud: "This is my Son, whom I love. Listen to him!"

⁸Suddenly, when they looked around, they no longer saw anyone with them except Jesus.

⁹As they were going down the mountain, Jesus gave them orders not to tell anyone what they had seen until the Son of Man had risen from the dead. ¹⁰They kept the matter to themselves, discussing what "rising from the dead" meant.

4. Why didn't Jesus take Peter's advice?

5. Describe a time when you experienced a spiritual high and your feelings when you came back down to earth.

6. How will this Bible study help you deal with your spiritual highs and lows?

Group Talk

1. If you could be on a spiritual high all the time, would you want to be? Why or why not?
2. What's good or bad about feeling guilty that our relationship with God isn't what it should be?
3. What helps you get over the inevitable letdown that comes after a fantastic retreat or youth conference or other spiritual high?

THE A.C.T.S. OF PRAYER

START HERE → *warm***UP**

In Touch with God

In "The Creation," a poem by James Weldon Johnson, God labors long and hard to create the land, the sea, the birds, the fish, the animals. And then God looks around and realizes that he is "lonely" still. The amazing world God created is absolutely perfect and beautiful, but that isn't enough for God. God wants a relationship with human beings.

Sure, we know that the Almighty Creator of heaven and earth doesn't really need to hang out with us. God is never "lonely" because God is complete in himself. God doesn't really need us for company (after all, heaven is full of angels, right?). Even so, God *wanted* and still wants a relationship with us. God enjoys our company! When you think about it, that's an amazing thing.

So, like a parent reaching out to hug a child, God reaches out to us. "Talk to me," God says, and then gives us specific instructions and examples on how to do just that. Trouble is, too often we tend to hold back. We're like Rambo: *Give me a Swiss army knife and I'll make it on my own.* We may not feel the need to pray, and so we back off. Sometimes we feel guilty about this, and that gives us even less desire to pray—and so the cycle continues.

We know better. We know a God who is willing to be part of our lives. We know an Almighty God who is totally able to do truly amazing things and who is our friend. This friend knows us better than we know ourselves. This friend knows that keeping in touch with him is exactly what we need.

In these meetings about prayer, we'll look at our prayer lives and how we can communicate better with the God who made us. Next time we'll introduce a way of praying called the A.C.T.S. of prayer.

1. If you wanted to get to know someone better, would you
   ___ avoid him as much as possible?
   ___ call her up from time to time?
   ___ ask his opinion about stuff?
   ___ talk mostly about the weather?
   ___ ask others about her?
   ___ set some time aside for him?
   ___ fall asleep when talking with her?
   ___ do something else:

2. What childhood memories do you associate with prayer?

3. What letter grade would you give your prayer life right now?

Matthew 6:5-15

1. As you read this passage, watch for Jesus' attitude toward those who pray for the wrong reasons.

2. What do you imagine is the tone of voice Jesus is using in this passage?

3. What directions does Jesus give about how to pray?

4. Why does Jesus immediately talk about forgiveness in verses 14 and 15?

5. How would you summarize what the disciples learned from this passage?

6. Mention one thing from this passage that you'll try to practice when you pray.

⁵"And when you pray, do not be like the hypocrites, for they love to pray standing in the synagogues and on the street corners to be seen by men. I tell you the truth, they have received their reward in full. ⁶But when you pray, go into your room, close the door and pray to your Father, who is unseen. Then your Father, who sees what is done in secret, will reward you. ⁷And when you pray, do not keep on babbling like pagans, for they think they will be heard because of their many words. ⁸Do not be like them, for your Father knows what you need before you ask him.

⁹"This, then, is how you should pray:
"'Our Father in heaven,
hallowed be your name,
¹⁰your kingdom come,
your will be done
        on earth as it is in heaven.
¹¹Give us today our daily bread.
¹²Forgive us our debts,
        as we also have forgiven our debtors.
¹³And lead us not into temptation,
but deliver us from the evil one.'

¹⁴"For if you forgive men when they sin against you, your heavenly Father will also forgive you. ¹⁵But if you do not forgive men their sins, your Father will not forgive your sins."

Group Talk

1. Share with each other when, where, and how you pray.
2. Share with each other the difficulties you have praying. Exchange ideas about how to deal with these difficulties.

START HERE ➔ *warm*UP

Adoration

In these meetings about prayer, we'll be following a familiar but helpful guide to praying: the A.C.T.S. of prayer. The first step of prayer in the A.C.T.S. method is adoration (praise). Adoration is followed by confession, thanksgiving, and supplication (asking for ourselves and others). Using A.C.T.S. for at least some of our prayers gives us a way to organize our time with God. It helps us include the same things in our prayers that Jesus taught his disciples to include in theirs.

Maybe you're already using A.C.T.S. in your prayers, and maybe not. Keep an open mind, and see what A.C.T.S. does for your prayer life.

Today we'll focus on "adoration." What does it mean to adore God when we pray? We usually don't think of God as "adorable." We might use that word to describe cuddly little babies and teddy bears, but not Almighty God! To "adore" someone or something is to love and admire that person or thing. To adore God, we need to stop and focus all our attention on him out of total respect and awe for who God is.

What happens when we do this? A couple of things. First, it puts us in a right frame of mind to pray. We stop and realize whose awesome presence we have entered. When we really focus on God, it puts perspective on our lives and our problems. Life doesn't look as bleak when we focus on God. Second, it's good for us to remember what a mighty God we serve. By praising God we gain a better idea of who God is.

1. A little game here. Everyone in the group closes their eyes except for the person who is "it." The person who is "it" must describe one member of the group to the others (what the person looks like, what he/she is wearing, other clues about things he/she does or is like). Everyone else needs to guess who the person is describing. Play this game with several people being "it." (If your group is really small, try describing someone the group would know outside of the group, like a teacher at school.)

2. Stop and read the left side of this page.

3. As a game like this goes on, people become better at describing others in the group. The same is true when we try to describe God when we pray, praising God for who he is and what he has done. We may not be very good now, but we improve with practice. Think about God and make a list of the names by which God is known; also list some of the great things God has done. Here are some examples:
   - knows everything about us
   - Creator of everything that is beautiful and good
   - the One who keeps this world going from day to day

Psalm 46

1. As you read, notice the difference between what life is like near God and what life is like away from God. What are some of the catastrophes that are happening away from God? Do these things fit our world? If you were writing this psalm today, what things might you mention that cause people to be afraid?

2. In the middle of all this disaster, how is God described in verses 1-7? Would these thoughts help you during a time when you're worried or afraid?

¹God is our refuge and strength,
  an ever-present help in trouble.
²Therefore we will not fear, though the earth give way
  and the mountains fall into the heart of the sea,
³though its waters roar and foam
  and the mountains quake with their surging.
⁴There is a river whose streams make glad the city of God,
  the holy place where the Most High dwells.
⁵God is within her, she will not fall;
  God will help her at break of day.
⁶Nations are in uproar, kingdoms fall;
  he lifts his voice, the earth melts.

⁷The LORD Almighty is with us;
  the God of Jacob is our fortress.

⁸Come and see the works of the LORD,
  the desolations he has brought on the earth.
⁹He makes wars cease to the ends of the earth;
  he breaks the bow and shatters the spear,
  he burns the shields with fire.
¹⁰"Be still, and know that I am God;
  I will be exalted among the nations,
  I will be exalted in the earth.

¹¹The LORD Almighty is with us;
  the God of Jacob is our fortress.

3. What picture of God do you get from verses 8-9?

4. Why does God want us to be still (v. 10)?

5. What in this psalm makes you want to praise God?

6. What will you take from this psalm into your life today?

Group Talk

1. Lots of bad stuff happens in this psalm. Yet the psalmist seems to have no problem trusting God. What gets in the way of our trusting God when things get bad?
2. What is the difference between thanking God and praising God?
3. Praising God and complimenting God may be rusty skills for us. Maybe it's because we don't do a very good job of praising each other. Discuss and come up with a plan of action as to how we can better compliment each other.

Confession

If we follow the A.C.T.S. method of praying, first we adore (praise) God, then we confess our sins. Whenever we think about how great God is and praise him for that greatness we can see how flawed we are. So confession after adoration makes sense. We need to confess our flaws to God.

Sometimes we kind of rattle off our confession, adding it to the end of our prayer like an afterthought: "Oh, and Lord, please forgive my many, many sins." Or maybe we've even said something like, "And forgive my sins of omission as well as commission," sweeping all our sins under the rug at once, so to speak.

What's wrong with being so vague about our sins? Simply this: if we aren't specific about our sins, we feel less guilt and shame, and we aren't as aware of our own weaknesses. It is much easier to say, "God, forgive my sins" than it is to say, "God, I told my parents I was going one place last night when I really went somewhere else. That makes me a hypocrite and a liar and I really need you to forgive me."

God is eager to forgive us. "If we confess our sins, he is faithful and just and will forgive us our sin" (1 John 1:9). That's good news for sinners like us! No matter how often we fall down into the dirt, God stands by to pick us up and clean us off. We can't get that forgiveness unless we ask for it, unless we confess our sins to our God.

Does this "easy" forgiveness mean we can just go out and sin some more? No way. You remember what Jesus said to the woman caught committing adultery: "Neither do I condemn you. Go now and leave your life of sin" (John 8:11).

1. Remember a time when you got caught doing something you shouldn't have been doing at school or at home or somewhere else. Share this event with the group if you can. Would your punishment have been greater or smaller if you had confessed it first?

2. Discuss what is easy and difficult about confession.

3. How do you feel towards someone who apologizes to you? How do you think God feels when we confess our sins?

Psalm 51:1-12

For the director of music. A psalm of David. When the prophet Nathan came to him after David had committed adultery with Bathsheba.

[1]Have mercy on me, O God,
    according to your unfailing love;
according to your great compassion
    blot out my transgressions.
[2]Wash away all my iniquity
    and cleanse me from my sin.

[3]For I know my transgressions,
    and my sin is always before me.
[4]Against you, you only, have I sinned
    and done what is evil in your sight,
so that you are proved right when you speak
    and justified when you judge.
[5]Surely I was sinful at birth,
    sinful from the time my mother conceived me.
[6]Surely you desire truth in the inner parts;
    you teach me wisdom in the inmost place.

[7]Cleanse me with hyssop, and I will be clean;
    wash me, and I will be whiter than snow.
[8]Let me hear joy and gladness;
    let the bones you have crushed rejoice.
[9]Hide your face from my sins
    and blot out all my iniquity.

[10]Create in me a pure heart, O God,
    and renew a steadfast spirit within me.
[11]Do not cast me from your presence
    or take your Holy Spirit from me.
[12]Restore to me the joy of your salvation
    and grant me a willing spirit, to sustain me.

1. As you read this psalm, note what David asks for (over a dozen things).

2. If you know the story behind this psalm (see heading), talk about it. What other sins (besides adultery) did David commit? How was David told about his sin? Was he forgiven? Punished? What happened to the child of David and Bathsheba?

3. Describe David's emotions as he writes/prays this psalm.

4. David says God desires "truth in the inner parts" (v. 6). What do you think that means?

5. Summarize what this prayer teaches you about confession and adoration (look for some praise lines in the psalm).

6. Pick a verse from the psalm that will help you pray and/or live the Christian life. Share your choice with others in your group.

Group Talk

1. What makes asking for forgiveness genuine? What makes it fake?
2. Have you ever asked someone to forgive you? What makes it difficult?
3. Do you need to ask forgiveness from someone? Perhaps talk to the group about how you should do it, without getting into specifics (or simply go out and do it).

START HERE ➤

*warm***UP**

Thanksgiving

Adoration . . . Confession . . . Thanksgiving (or just plain thanks, if you prefer). The word "thanksgiving" probably brings to mind that holiday when we get to eat all the turkey and stuffing we can handle and, more importantly, we get two days off from school. Sometimes it's easy to forget the actual intent of the day: to pause and reflect on everything God has done for us.

Psalm 103:2 says, "Praise the LORD, O my soul, and forget not all his benefits." And that's exactly what we should do when we pray: reflect on everything God has done for us and then give thanks for those things. Remember, though, that just feeling grateful for what God has done for us and actually thanking God are two different things! We humans want others to say thank you when we do something for them; it isn't enough just for them to feel grateful but not say anything. God also wants to hear us say, "Thank you, God!"

So let's say you're having a truly rotten day and you're a long, long way from feeling grateful, let alone saying thank you. You got mad at your mom, you didn't get invited to that party, you forgot the last third of the math test, you missed your ride home from school, and so on. On days like that—and when far more serious things go wrong—it's tempting to think of everything God has not done for us!

The apostle Paul reminds us to "give thanks in all circumstances, for this is God's will in Christ Jesus" (1 Thess. 5:18). Focus on the incredible number of good things God has done for you, not on those things—for whatever reason—God hasn't done.

"Thank you, God, for . . . "

1. When writing a thank-you note, do you
   ___ have one ready in case you need it?
   ___ write it quickly so you don't forget to do it?
   ___ keep reminding yourself that you really ought to get around to it and then feel guilty when you don't?
   ___ What? A thank-you note? What's that?

2. Recall a time when you did something for someone and he or she didn't give you word one of thanks. Describe the incident and tell how it made you feel.

3. Is there someone who's long overdue in receiving thanks from you for something?

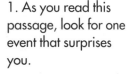

Luke 17:11-19

1. As you read this passage, look for one event that surprises you.

2. Why do you suppose nine of the lepers did not return to give thanks? Why do you suppose the one leper did return to give thanks?

3. What does Jesus question about the event? Why does the writer seem to think it is important to point out that the returning leper is a Samaritan?

¹¹Now on his way to Jerusalem, Jesus traveled along the border between Samaria and Galilee. ¹²As he was going into a village, ten men who had leprosy met him. They stood at a distance ¹³and called in a loud voice, "Jesus, Master, have pity on us!"

¹⁴When he saw them, he said, "Go, show yourselves to the priests." And as they went, they were cleansed.

¹⁵One of them, when he saw he was healed, came back, praising God in a loud voice. ¹⁶He threw himself at Jesus' feet and thanked him—and he was a Samaritan.

¹⁷Jesus asked, "Were not all ten cleansed? Where are the other nine? ¹⁸Was no one found to return and give praise to God except this foreigner?" ¹⁹Then he said to him, "Rise and go; your faith has made you well."

4. If you had been one of the lepers, would you have returned to give thanks? Explain.

5. Share a couple of things for which you want to thank God.

6. What will this passage make you think about today?

Group Talk

1. What kind of attitude do we learn when we are constantly appreciative?
2. What does it mean to be self-centered? What does that do to our relationship with God and with those around us?

5 THE A.C.T.S. OF PRAYER

START HERE → *warm*UP

Supplication

The last of the A.C.T.S. of prayer is supplication. To "supplicate" is to humbly ask for something. So this part of our prayer simply involves humbly bringing our requests—for ourselves and others—to God.

There may be times when we are guilty of too much "supplication," when God becomes a giant Santa Claus and every day is Christmas (imagine treating a rich friend like that!). When we pray, we also need to differentiate between the things we need and the things we want. It's fine to pray for things we want, as long as these things are not clearly outside of God's revealed will (like praying that your competitor for first chair in the trumpet section develops a severe sore throat the night before tryouts). That's a lame example, but you get the point.

God wants us to ask him for all kinds of things—for ourselves and especially for others. (Remember that the Lord's Prayer says, "Give *us* today our daily bread.") Listen to Paul's advice: "In everything, by prayer and petition, with thanksgiving, present your requests to God" (Phil. 4:6). So go ahead, ask!

But how do we know if what we are asking for is good for us? If you're unsure, say something like this: "Dear God, I have this request, and I'm not sure it's right for me, but you have asked me to present my requests. If you have something better in mind for me, please do it your way and help me to trust you."

Making lists for this time of prayer can be helpful. Keeping them under headings like "friends," "family," and "work" can help you remain consistent in your prayer life and see how God responds to your prayers.

This is the final meeting on the A.C.T.S. approach. Has it helped you? While it's obviously not the only way to pray, it is definitely a good, biblical approach. Stick with it and see.

1. What plant best describes your prayer life right now (and explain why):
___giant redwood
___clinging vine
___immense oak
___cactus
___poison sumac
___bamboo
___plastic decorative bush
___scuzzy mold growing in the bottom of your shower
___ other:

2. How do you feel about asking God for things for yourself? For others?

3. Do you tend to think too big or too small in your prayer requests?

53

Philippians 4:4-7

[4]Rejoice in the Lord always. I will say it again: Rejoice! [5]Let your gentleness be evident to all. The Lord is near. [6]Do not be anxious about anything, but in everything, by prayer and petition with thanksgiving, present your requests to God. [7]And the peace of God, which transcends all understanding, will guard your hearts and your minds in Christ Jesus.

Matthew 7:7

"Ask and it will be given to you; seek and you will find; knock and the door will be opened to you."

1. As you read this, look for three commands that Paul gives us.

2. What are we to do always (v. 4)? What does that mean?

3. Instead of worrying about something, what does Paul say we should do? What does that tell you about the kind of things God wants you to ask for?

4. Describe what "the peace of God" (v. 7) means to you.

5. Share an example of something that you asked God for and were given (Matt. 7:7).

6. What will you try to practice based on what we talked about today?

Group Talk

1. Is it better to ask for world peace and an end to hunger, or for good relationships and a day that goes well?
2. When does God give us what we want?

With Parents

The God we serve is a God of relationships. When you stop to think about it, the three persons of the Trinity are in a kind of holy relationship. Through the Trinity, God is in relationship with himself. God also created human beings because God wanted to be in relationship with us (not because God needed us). We, in turn, serve God through the relationships we have with God, with others, with God's creation. In the next six meetings we'll take a close look at some of these relationships.

Which relationship shaped you more than any other? Probably the one between you and your parent or parents. If your parents are Democrats, chances are better than 50-50 that you are too. If your parents go to church, you're far more likely to attend church than if they did not. If your parents model careful use of this world's resources, you'll likely reflect their love for creation. Not that it always happens this way—conservative parents can and do raise very liberal kids! But for better or for worse, much of who we are and who we will become is shaped by our parents. For that reason, God is careful to define how parents should treat their children and how children should act towards their parents.

This bond between parents and children has increasingly come under attack. Too many parents don't spend time with kids; too many kids are too busy with their own activities to talk much to Mom or Dad. Relationships that God intended to last a lifetime don't. There are many broken families in our broken world.

Today's Bible study will get us talking about our relationship with our parents—what God expects, what's good, what's not so good, and what we can do about it.

1. What's one thing parents generally do that you like and appreciate? One thing you wish they wouldn't do?

2. Here is a list of troubles that frequently surface in families. You can probably relate to some but not all of them. Mark three that bother you the most.*
   ___ chores
   ___ discipline
   ___ unequal treatment of siblings
   ___ curfews
   ___ stepparents
   ___ lack of respect
   ___ lack of privacy
   ___ not enough Snickerdoodles
   ___ parents divorced or currently getting divorce
   ___ parents fight
   ___ homework/grades
   ___ strict parental decisions on music and friends
   ___ non-Christian parents
   ___ Christian parents
   ___ parents gone all the time
   ___ parents upset about . . .
   ___ going to church
   ___ too little allowance
   ___ use of the car
   ___ dating (or lack of) relationships
   ___ other:

3. Go back over the three items you've checked. Write in the margin the following letters to indicate who you think causes the problem or whose problem it is.
   • M = Mine. I cause them.
   • P = Parents cause them.
   • B = Both cause them.
   Share one item from your list with others in your group.

*The author is indebted to Serendipity House and its excellent small group materials for the approach used in questions 2 and 3.

Deuteronomy 5:16

Honor your father and your mother, as the LORD your God has commanded you, so that you may live long and that it may go well with you in the land the LORD your God is giving you.

Ephesians 6:1-4

¹Children, obey your parents in the Lord, for this is right. ²"Honor your father and your mother"—which is the first commandment with a promise— ³"that it may go well with you and that you may enjoy long life on the earth."

⁴Fathers, do not exasperate your children; instead, bring them up in the training and instruction of the Lord.

1. As you read, look at the verbs that describe how children and parents should respond to each other.

2. How would you define "honor"? What does it mean to honor parents? May we ever not honor our parents?

3. Why, according to these passages, should children honor their parents?

4. How would you, in your own home, define "exasperate"? Give some examples.

5. God wants parents to teach their kids to love him (v. 4). How do you think this should be done? Not be done?

6. What conversation might you have with your parents after studying this text?

Group Talk

1. Who keeps the peace in your house?
2. Go back to the Warm-up exercise, question 2. Give each other some practical advice about how to solve these problems.

With Brothers and Sisters

We are called children of God. That makes us brothers and sisters in Christ. Initially, this sounds pretty warm and wonderful. But wait a minute: this "brother and sister" thing may not exactly be heaven on earth.

Rare are the brothers and sisters who always get along (even when Mom and Dad aren't home). Kids in the same family tend to argue over a whole bunch of little things: what program to watch on TV, who has to baby-sit the younger kids, who gets to use the home computer, and so on. There's apparently no end to the ways sibs can annoy each other—even when, down deep, they love each other.

That's not exactly a new problem. The Bible, for example, tells the story of Jacob and Esau, twins who couldn't stand each other. Esau liked to hunt and was favored by his father. Jacob liked to cook and was favored by his mother. One day Esau came in from the fields, famished, and Jacob talked him into giving up his inheritance rights as the firstborn, in exchange for a bowl or two of the stew he had just cooked. Later, Jacob and his mother tricked old Isaac into giving Jacob, not Esau, the blessing. After that, Esau looked for ways to kill his brother (Gen. 27:41). So Jacob fled to his uncle Laban, married Laban's two daughters, had eleven sons, and generally prospered. One day, Jacob decided to take his family back home to Canaan. On the way, he heard that Esau was coming toward him—with four hundred armed men . . .

Jacob and Esau didn't get along too well, it seems (today's Bible study will tell us how their clash turned out). Be that as it may, for those of us who have been *blessed* with brothers and sisters, God calls us to love them!

That call to love our siblings isn't new. Long ago, the apostle Paul said: "If anyone does not provide for his relatives, and especially his immediate family, he has denied the faith and is worse than an unbeliever" (1 Tim. 5:8).

Brothers and sisters. If we've got 'em, God tells us to love 'em.

1. What does your brother or sister (or someone else close to you if you don't have siblings) do that really annoys you? Multiple answers permissible!

2. OK, so something your brother or sister (or someone else close to you) does really annoys you. Do you usually
   ___ say nothing, just get mad inside?
   ___ avoid him or her?
   ___ give him or her the silent treatment?
   ___ tell all your friends (and your brother's or sister's friends) what a jerk he or she is?
   ___ complain to a parent?
   ___ use threats?
   ___ use physical force?
   ___ try to talk out the problem with him or her?
   ___ do something else? What?

3. Why is it that family relationships can be more difficult than friend-to-friend relationships?

Excerpts from Genesis 32-33

[7] In great fear and distress Jacob divided the people who were with him into two groups. . . . [8] He thought, "If Esau comes and attacks one group, the group that is left may escape."

[9] Then Jacob prayed . . . [11] "Save me . . . from the hand of my brother Esau, for I am afraid he will come and attack me, and also the mothers with their children."

[As an additional precaution, Jacob also sent wave after wave of gifts to his brother Esau.]

[1] Jacob looked up and there was Esau, coming with his four hundred men; so he divided the children among Leah, Rachel and the two maidservants. . . . [3] He himself went on ahead and bowed down to the ground seven times as he approached his brother.

[4] But Esau ran to meet Jacob and embraced him; he threw his arms around his neck and kissed him. And they wept. [5] Then Esau looked up and saw the women and children. "Who are these with you?" he asked.

Jacob answered, "They are the children God has graciously given your servant."

[6] Then the maidservants and their children approached and bowed down. [7] Next, Leah and her children came and bowed down. Last of all came Joseph and Rachel, and they too bowed down.

[8] Esau asked, "What do you mean by all those droves (animals) I met?"

"To find favor in your eyes, my lord," he said.

[9] But Esau said, "I already have plenty, my brother. Keep what you have for yourself."

[10] "No, please!" said Jacob. "If I have found favor in your eyes, accept this gift from me. For to see your face is like seeing the face of God, now that you have received me favorably." [11] And because Jacob insisted, Esau accepted it. . . .

[16] So that day, Esau started on his way back to Seir. [17] Jacob, however, went to Succoth. . . .

1. As you read this, imagine yourself as Jacob, seeing his brother Esau coming with four hundred men. What would your thoughts and feelings be?

2. Now imagine yourself as Esau. What would you be thinking and feeling?

3. What did Jacob do to prepare the way for reconciliation? Esau had wanted to kill Jacob when Jacob stole the blessing (some twenty years in the past). What do you think changed his mind?

4. Suppose you and a brother or sister (or someone else close to you) really went at it over something. You realize now that you were mostly at fault. You said some truly nasty things and so did your sibling. How could you set this situation straight? See if you can pick up an idea or two from Jacob's example.

5. What can you learn from Esau's example about how to act when a brother or sister (or someone else) has really offended you and then seeks reconciliation?

6. Talk about a relationship with a brother or sister (or someone else close to you) that you would like to improve (even if it's pretty good already). What might you do to change the relationship for the better?

Group Talk

1. Jacob asked God for help when meeting Esau. What part can prayer play in our relationship with siblings? What can we pray for?

2. If there are kids in the group who don't have brothers or sisters, invite them to talk about some of the advantages and disadvantages of being an only child.

3 RELATIONSHIPS

With Friends

Friends are one of God's greatest gifts to us. Friends are people who want to share in each other's lives, both the good and the bad. Friends can model Jesus for each other; they can question and affirm each other about their beliefs and actions.

Unfortunately, what can be a very positive experience can be a very negative experience as well. Friends can move away or, worse yet, change. People who have been very close in the past may suddenly lack interest in continuing the friendship. Especially in high school, people are continually redefining who they want to be. Friendships can dissolve quickly and leave hurt feelings.

The book of Proverbs has some fine things to say about friendships. Here are a few samples:

- A gossip separates close friends (16:28).
- A friend loves at all times (17:17).
- A man of many companions may come to ruin; but there is a friend who sticks closer than a brother (18:24).
- Wounds from a friend can be trusted (27:6).
- Do not forsake your friend (27:10).

God created us to be in friendship with others, to give and receive the love of Jesus through our friends. This may mean confronting our friends when they screw up, or accepting constructive criticism when we screw up. Both acts are difficult but necessary among Christian friends.

Jesus says, "My command is this: Love each other as I have loved you. Greater love has no one than this, that he lay down his life for his friends. You are my friends if you do what I command" (John 15:12-14).

1. Mention a real life friendship or a friendship you've read about or seen in the movies or on TV that you think is a pretty good example of what being friends means.

2. Describe one kind or caring thing a friend did for you.

3. What qualities do you look for in a friend?

1 Samuel 18:1-4

¹After David had finished talking with Saul, Jonathan became one in spirit with David, and he loved him as himself. ²From that day Saul kept David with him and he did not let him return to his father's house. ³And Jonathan made a covenant with David because he loved him as himself. ⁴Jonathan took off the robe he was wearing and gave it to David, along with his tunic, and even his sword, his bow and his belt.

1 Samuel 19:1-6

¹Saul told his son Jonathan and all the attendants to kill David. But Jonathan was very fond of David ²and warned him, "My father Saul is looking for a chance to kill you. Be on your guard tomorrow morning; go into hiding and stay there. ³I will go out and stand with my father in the field where you are. I'll speak to him about you and will tell you what I find out."

⁴Jonathan spoke well of David to Saul his father and said to him, "Let not the king do wrong to his servant David; he has not wronged you, and what he has done has benefited you greatly. ⁵He took his life in his hands when he killed the Philistine. The LORD won a great victory for all Israel, and you saw it and were glad. Why then would you do wrong to an innocent man like David by killing him for no reason?"

⁶Saul listened to Jonathan and took this oath, "As surely as the LORD lives, David will not be put to death."

1. As you read this, look for words that describe how Jonathan felt about his friend David. Review them with the group.

2. How was David and Jonathan's friendship tested? Have you ever taken a stand for a friend, or vice versa?

3. Circle the things that Jonathan does for David in these passages. What did Jonathan do for David that you wish someone would do for you?

4. How did Jonathan honor his father even though he disobeyed him?

5. David's life was spared through his friendship with Jonathan. Talk about some of the benefits of friendships that you've experienced.

6. What new ideas or good reminders did you take from today's Bible study that could affect your friendships in the future?

Group Talk

1. Your friend is doing something you think might be bad for him or her (dating the wrong person, drinking, lying to parents). How do you confront your friend? What risks might you have to take for the sake of your friend? (If your group feels like it, act out some situations that show appropriate and inappropriate ways to confront a friend.)

2. How do you confront a friend who is not treating you well?

3. Talk about any other questions about friendship that the group would like to discuss.

4 RELATIONSHIPS

START HERE → *warm* UP

With the Opposite Sex

In his infinite wisdom, God created a bond between men and women. This, of course, extends to young men and women, to boys and girls all the way down to freshies and the rest of the food chain. It's interesting how the male/female relationship goes through stages. Your kid sister might think boys are icky and creepy; your kid brother might think girls are sissies. Fortunately, these stages pass quickly, and before long, our God-given attraction to the opposite sex kicks in with an intensity that's hard to ignore.

The chemistry in all this male/female stuff is extremely powerful. It can lead to marriage and some of God's greatest gifts to us: intimacy, sex, children, companionship. The downside is that falling out of these relationships ranks as one of the most painful experiences we face.

Given the positive and negative power of male/female relationships, it seems obvious that before (and during) our relationships we do some serious thinking. We need to remember who we are: people created in the image of our God. Guys and girls are accountable for treating their counterparts with respect, not just as body parts. We are to put each other's needs ahead of our own. That may mean breaking off a poor relationship, or choosing not to date at all if we feel we don't want to accept the responsibilities that come with it.

Maybe you're not all that interested at the moment in this topic; maybe other things claim your time and attention. That's great—be your own person. Date and commit to a relationship when you're ready to. But meanwhile, it doesn't hurt to prepare for the possibilities. Think carefully about the kind of person you're looking for in a dating partner. Set some standards and limits while clear, objective thinking is still possible. And while you wait, remember that God is still in control. God created us with our needs and desires; God has a plan for our lives. It's up to us to live each day fully trusting that God will do what is best for us.

1. How would you like to be described by persons of the opposite sex? Males make one list; females make one list. Then compare.

2. What does it mean to you to be respected? How do you want to be treated? Again, you may want to do this in two groups, males and females. Then compare notes.

3. Do you think God's will for male/female relationships is generally quite clear, or is it fuzzy and debatable?

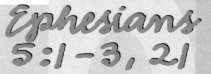

Ephesians 4:1-3, 17, 19-20

[1]As a prisoner for the Lord, then, I urge you to live a life worthy of the calling you have received. [2]Be completely humble and gentle; be patient, bearing with one another in love. [3]Make every effort to keep the unity of the Spirit through the bond of peace.

[17]So I tell you this, and insist on it in the Lord, that you must no longer live as the Gentiles do, in the futility of their thinking. . . . [19]Having lost all sensitivity, they have given themselves over to sensuality so as to indulge in every kind of impurity, with a continual lust for more.

[20]You, however, did not come to know Christ that way.

Ephesians 5:1-3, 21

[1]Be imitators of God, therefore, as dearly loved children [2]and live a life of love, just as Christ loved us and gave himself up for us. . . .

[3]But among you there must not be even a hint of sexual immorality, or of any kind of impurity, or of greed, because these are improper for God's holy people.

[21]Submit to one another out of reverence for Christ.

1. As you read this, notice the sharp contrast between selfish and unselfish behavior. After reading, make a list of words in this passage that describe a selfish, un-Christian way of relating to the opposite sex. Make another list of words from the passage that describe a selfless, Christian way of relating to the opposite sex.

2. What does it mean to "imitate God" in your relationships?

3. How can we live without a hint of any kind of impurity? Is this really possible?

4. What does the word "submit" mean in a relationship? (Not what you might think!)

5. What are some of the really good things that can result from a relationship that honors God and respects the other person?

6. Share one insight or good reminder that you picked up from today's Bible study or discussion.

group Talk

1. If you were dating someone and you found out that the person no longer wanted to date you, would you want that person to tell you? How?
2. Is kissing someone you're not dating, just for the fun of it, OK?
3. After reading these passages, just how much of a role should "being physical" play in high school relationships?

With Myself

The Bible never really talks about the need to love ourselves. This fact appears to be taken for granted. But how often do we see the God-given gift of self-worth thrown away? How many times have you heard kids put themselves down for not being thin enough, smart enough, athletic enough, or just plain not good enough when compared to classmates or to the impossible standards set by our culture? Other kids, it seems, are always thinner, better-looking, better jocks, better students than we are. Others have nicer clothes, live in nicer houses, drive cooler cars, have more friends than we ever will.

Whoa! What are we doing to ourselves? While some comparing is normal and good, it's just not healthy to be forever measuring ourselves by others. And it's particularly inappropriate for Christians. Why? It's simple: we are God's children, each one with unique looks, gifts, personalities. When we constantly compare ourselves to others or to the standards set by our culture, it's like saying to God, "Uh, how come you didn't make me as smart or as beautiful or as athletic or as cool as he or she is?" Remember, we are exactly the way God created us, the way God wants us to be! We need to constantly remind ourselves that our God loves us and cares for us—*as we are.* Appearance, material possessions, and ability are not the basis of our self-worth.

Once we accept ourselves, we free up time to think about others and to give them the gift of accepting themselves. As pastor Jake Herrema once said, "God is calling us to contribute to one another's self-esteem. There is no room for judging, put-downs, constant criticizing, inappropriate expectations, comparisons, and basing our expectations of others on what they do rather than who they are. God grants us the gift of worth. One's self-worth is not earned, but given."

1. What do you think when people stare at you?

2. Go around the circle, focusing on one person at a time. For each person, others in the group should mention one or more essential qualities (gifts) this person has been given by God. (For example, he or she is really organized; shows a lot of care and concern for others; is a good leader.)

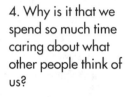

Matthew 10:29-31

29"Are not two sparrows sold for a penny? Yet not one of them will fall to the ground apart from the will of your Father. 30And even the very hairs of your head are all numbered. 31So don't be afraid; you are worth more than many sparrows."

Luke 12:22-26

22Then Jesus said to his disciples: "Therefore I tell you, do not worry about your life, what you will eat; or about your body, what you will wear. 23Life is more than food, and the body more than clothes. 24Consider the ravens: They do not sow or reap, they have no storeroom or barn; yet God feeds them. And how much more valuable you are than birds! 25Who of you by worrying can add a single hour to his life? 26Since you cannot do this very little thing, why do you worry about the rest?"

1. As you read these passages, consider what God must think of you.

2. In the Matthew passage, what does God seem to know?

3. According to the Luke passage, what are we not supposed to worry about?

4. Why is it that we spend so much time caring about what other people think of us?

5. If you're up to it, share a thought about an area in your life where you feel inadequate or have some self-doubt. Afterward, read the Matthew passage for confirmation of what God thinks of us.

6. If there's a single thought from the Bible study or discussion that you'll take with you this week, what is it?

group Talk

1. Why do we so often focus on our faults instead of our strengths?
2. Self-esteem is not easy to increase, even when we focus on God's acceptance of us. What can we do to build up our sense of self-worth?
3. What are some specific ways we can help build up each other's sense of self-worth?

6 RELATIONSHIPS

START HERE →

1. Why does Hawaii have interstate highways?

2. Make a list of words that describe God.

3. Make a list of words that describe a good friend. Compare the two lists.

With God

God created us to be in relationship with him—not out of loneliness or a desire for company, but because God loves us and wants us to share in that love.

It's sad, but often we find ourselves ignoring this relationship. We give God a tiny part of our busy days, maybe because we feel we don't have that much time to give, or we just don't want to pay much attention to God. And the longer we stay away from God, the harder it is to get close to God again.

That's not the way it's supposed to be. Our growing relationship with God should be the most important aspect of our lives. Listen to this: the Almighty God of heaven and earth wants to spend some time with us—with you and me! Like a good friend, God is *eager* to hear from us! God values our company. Can we really say we don't have space for God in our lives?

Martin Luther once said, "I have so much to do, if I don't pray for three or four hours first, it'll never get done." Of course, he said it in German, but you get the gist. Staying in touch with God isn't a luxury to be squeezed in if we have the time; it's an absolute necessity. *Especially* when we're feeling time-stressed and when the demands of school, work, family, and our social life are threatening to drive us up the wall. It is precisely then, says Luther, that we need to stay in touch with God—even if it means getting up a little earlier or passing up our favorite TV show or taking time from our busy day to talk about God (as you are doing right now!).

Getting to know God—so that we may better worship and serve him—is our chief purpose in this life. In fact, it's what eternal life is all about too. "Now this is eternal life: that they may know you, the only true God" (John 17:3).

Luke 10:38-42

1. As you read this passage, notice the difference between Mary's and Martha's response to Jesus.

2. Why was Martha upset? Can you understand her feelings? (Does anything like this ever happen with your brothers or sisters?)

3. What is the "one thing" that "is needed" which Jesus speaks of in verse 42?

[38]As Jesus and his disciples were on their way, he came to a village where a woman named Martha opened her home to him. [39]She had a sister called Mary, who sat at the Lord's feet listening to what he said. [40]But Martha was distracted by all the preparations that had to be made. She came to him and asked, "Lord, don't you care that my sister has left me to do the work by myself? Tell her to help me!"

[41]"Martha, Martha," the Lord answered, "you are worried and upset about many things, [42]but only one thing is needed. Mary has chosen what is better, and it will not be taken away from her."

4. Who are you more like, Martha or Mary? Explain.

5. What gets in the way of your sitting down and spending time with God?

6. Share with each other what you will put into practice from this passage this week.

group Talk

1. What do you include in your personal devotions?
2. Brainstorm some ideas to help overcome some of the obstacles that get in the way of spending quality time with God mentioned in question 5, above.

START HERE →

*warm*UP

Called to Serve

Studying for tests, writing a paper, doing assignments, flipping burgers, waiting on tables, washing cars, delivering pizza, mopping floors, moving the dust around your room, shoveling snow, cutting the lawn, repairing the car, using the computer, doing a service project with your youth group . . . the list goes on. Work. It consumes much of our lives. Sometimes it's fun, sometimes like getting a root canal. Always it takes our time and effort.

So it's no surprise that sometimes it's hard for us to get excited about (and find time for) the work we're called to do as Christians. The fancy name for this work is service. We're called to serve God and others. Sure, Jesus came to earth to save us. He wants a relationship with us. But Jesus didn't just save us so he could hang out with us for eternity. He saved us so we could be agents of change in our neighborhoods and schools and even in our small groups.

Huh? How's that again? Agents of change? Right. Jesus came to transform our world, to bring in the kingdom of God. As Mark 10:45 says, "For even the Son of Man did not come to be served, but to serve, and to give his life as a ransom for many." Jesus wants us—his followers—to be servants too.

For the next four meetings, we'll talk together about what being a servant really involves. It's what we're called to be.

1. Describe a job or something else you had to do that was the pits, the absolute bottom of the barrel, something they couldn't pay you enough to do full time for the rest of your life.

2. On a scale of 1 to 10 (1 = a piece of cake; 10 = mission impossible), how would you rate the job of being a Christian today?

3. Do you think Jesus, the Son of God, thought of himself as a servant as he worked among people on earth? Why or why not?

Philippians 2:1-11
(The Message)

If you've gotten anything at all out of following Christ, if his love has made any difference in your life, if being in a community of the Spirit means anything to you, if you have a heart, if you *care*—then do me a favor: Agree with each other, love each other, be deep-spirited friends. Don't push your way to the front; don't sweet-talk your way to the top. Put yourself aside, and help others get ahead. Don't be obsessed with getting your own advantage. Forget yourselves long enough to lend a helping hand.

Think of yourselves the way Christ Jesus thought of himself. He had equal status with God but didn't think so much of himself that he had to cling to the advantages of that status no matter what. Not at all. When the time came, he set aside the privileges of deity and took on the status of a slave, became *human!* Having become human, he stayed human. It was an incredibly humbling process. He didn't claim special privileges. Instead, he lived a selfless, obedient life, and then died a selfless, obedient death—and the worst kind of death at that: a crucifixion.

Because of that obedience, God lifted him high and honored him far beyond anyone or anything, ever, so that all created beings in heaven and on earth—even those long ago dead and buried—will bow in worship before this Jesus Christ, and call out in praise that he is the Master of all, to the glorious honor of God the Father.

1. As you read this, look for advice on how we should treat each other and how Christ is our model for service.

2. Suppose you had to make an advertising slogan based on Paul's advice in the first paragraph. What could it be?

3. What part of the servant life do you think was most difficult for Jesus? Why? What to you is most difficult or demanding about being a servant?

4. What's the difference between being humble (using your gifts to help others) and being a doormat?

5. Because Jesus humbled himself and became a servant, God "lifted him high and honored him far beyond anyone or anything." Talk about the rewards of serving others. If possible, bring in your own experiences.

6. Pick a line from today's Scripture that you will carry in your mind and try to practice. Share your line with the group.

Group Talk

1. What would life be like in your family or with your friends or at work if everyone followed the advice from the end of the first paragraph of the passage?
2. Why is it that we are always so easily offended or that we feel wronged?
3. What's your attitude—right now—about all this servant stuff?

2 SERVICE

For the Least of These

Some people are easy to serve: our friends for whom we enjoy doing things; a favorite coach who asks us to work out at six in the morning; a needy person who thanks us profusely for painting his house; a friendly youth pastor who needs help serving a spaghetti supper at church, and so on. That kind of service is fun and rewarding.

But there are others whom we'd like to avoid, let alone serve: the employer who yells at us or never says we're doing a good job; the teacher who thinks his course is the only one we need to prepare for; the super-critical brother or sister or parent; the homeless person badgering us for a handout, and so on.

In some ways, being a servant for God seems like a pretty good deal. A servant to the most high King! Not bad! Trouble is, we're also called to serve the ordinary folks around us, and that doesn't seem at all as romantic or noble as serving a king. In fact, it is exactly in serving those who are difficult to love that we come to mirror the image of Christ most completely. Jesus, you remember, served one man who later denied him and another man who betrayed him. And he gave his life that *whoever* believes in him shall not perish but have eternal life (John 3:16).

"If you love those who love you, what credit is that to you?" asks Luke. He then reminds us to love our enemies and do good to them (Luke 6:32, 35). We're called to serve all kinds of people. Some are easy to serve, some are not.

Jesus speaks some pretty blunt words in Matthew 5:41: "If someone forces you to go one mile, go with him two miles." That's service.

1. Right now, my clothes at home are
   ___ in piles all over my bedroom, regardless of color.
   ___ in piles all over my bedroom, by color.
   ___ hanging neatly in my closet.
   ___ other:

2. Remember a time someone was kind to you in a totally unexpected way. What surprised you about this?

Matthew 25:31-40

1. As you read this parable about judgment day at the end of time, notice what Jesus thinks is important to do.

2. What kind of people are being served in Jesus' parable? What does that tell you about our service?

3. Why, according to this parable, should we serve others?

[31]"When the Son of Man comes in his glory, and all the angels with him, he will sit on his throne in heavenly glory. [32]All the nations will be gathered before him, and he will separate the people one from another as a shepherd separates the sheep from the goats. [33]He will put the sheep on his right and the goats on his left.

[34]"Then the King will say to those on his right, 'Come, you who are blessed by my Father; take your inheritance, the kingdom prepared for you since the creation of the world. [35]For I was hungry and you gave me something to eat, I was thirsty and you gave me something to drink, I was a stranger and you invited me in, [36]I needed clothes and you clothed me, I was sick and you looked after me, I was in prison and you came to visit me.'

[37]"Then the righteous will answer him, 'Lord, when did we see you hungry and feed you, or thirsty and give you something to drink? [38]When did we see you a stranger and invite you in, or needing clothes and clothe you? [39]When did we see you sick or in prison and go to visit you?'

[40]"The King will reply, 'I tell you the truth, whatever you did for one of the least of these brothers of mine, you did for me.'"

4. In our world today, what kinds of people might be identified as "the least of Jesus' brothers and sisters"?

5. Why aren't the righteous aware of their service to Jesus?

6. Think of one person whom you feel you could do a better job of serving this week.

Group Talk

1. How does this discussion about judgment day and separating the sheep from the goats make you feel?

2. Is Jesus teaching us that we are saved by what we do? Why or why not?

Wash Those Feet!

I
Me
Mine
Myself

Chuck Swindoll, in his book *Improving Your Serve,* writes about this pyramid of service. What gets in the way of our serving others? asks Swindoll. His answer: our own selves. When we put our own needs first, when we take offense, when we want more . . . we find it difficult to serve.

Serving is an attitude that we cultivate and discipline into our minds over a period of time. It's not as if we can just promise ourselves, *OK, from now on I'm going to think about putting other people first.* That's a good resolution, but will it really change us? Can we suddenly begin to live an unselfish life just by deciding to do so? It's a little like saying, *OK, from now on I'm going to be the teenage Michael Jordan.* But the next day we find we're having considerable trouble leaping three feet off the floor and slam-dunking with our backs to the basket.

There's a better, more realistic way: go for the goal but take smaller steps. Instead of saying, *Starting right now, I'm going to be the Mother Teresa of City High,* you could say, *From now on, I'll clean up the trash on the floor around my locker instead of letting the janitor do it.* Then do it. And when you succeed, take another small step.

Jesus gave us the example for this in a moment of humble service that shocked his disciples to their socks, so to speak. Then he said, "Now go do for others what I've done for you."

John 13:2-8, 12-15

[2]The evening meal was being served, and the devil had already prompted Judas Iscariot, son of Simon, to betray Jesus. [3]Jesus knew that the Father had put all things under his power, and that he had come from God and was returning to God; [4]so he got up from the meal, took off his outer clothing, and wrapped a towel around his waist. [5]After that, he poured water into a basin and began to wash his disciples' feet, drying them with the towel that was wrapped around him.

[6]He came to Simon Peter, who said to him, "Lord, are you going to wash my feet?"

[7]Jesus replied, "You do not realize now what I am doing, but later you will understand."

[8]"No," said Peter. "You shall never wash my feet."

Jesus answered, "Unless I wash you, you have no part with me. . . ."

[12]When he had finished washing their feet, he put on his clothes and returned to his place. "Do you understand what I have done for you?" he asked them. [13]"You call me 'Teacher' and 'Lord,' and rightly so, for that is what I am. [14]Now that I, your Lord and Teacher, have washed your feet, you also should wash one another's feet. [15]I have set you an example that you should do as I have done for you."

James 2:14-17

[14]What good is it, my brothers, if a man claims to have faith but has no deeds? Can such faith save him? [15]Suppose a brother or sister is without clothes and daily food. [16]If one of you says to him, "Go, I wish you well; keep warm and well fed," but does nothing about his physical needs, what good is it? [17]In the same way, faith by itself, if it is not accompanied by action, is dead.

---

1. As you read this, think of how you would have reacted to Jesus' act of service.

2. What kind of service did Jesus perform? Who usually did this? Transfer this act into our culture. What similar kind of service would Jesus do for us today?

3. Why did Jesus wash his disciples' feet? Why does he make such an obvious point of it (vv. 14-15)?

4. Do you think you would have reacted as Peter did? Why or why not?

5. What kinds of things can we do for others that would be similar to Jesus washing his disciples feet? See James 2 for some ideas, but add your own as well.

6. Think of a simple act of service you will commit to doing. Share your idea with others in your group.

---

group Talk

1. According to James, what is the measure of the depth (or shallowness) of our faith? Talk about how your faith measures up against this standard.

2. Talk about an experience of serving others in some small way. What did you do? What motivated you to do it? How was your act of service received? Were you glad you did it?

Excel in Giving

A high school student donates one of his healthy kidneys to a sister who needs it to live; another teen submits to the painful procedure of donating bone marrow to help a family member fight leukemia; an entire basketball team takes turns caring for a teammate's sick brother after school; a teen participates in a Friendship program and tutors someone with mental impairments; a group of high school kids clean up a local stream or highway; another group gives their Saturday morning to work in their church's food pantry.

Giving—of our time, effort, and money—goes on every day all around us. Your group can probably come up with many more examples. It's great to see the amount of giving that goes on in our high schools, churches, and communities.

Giving of all kinds gets easier when we take the focus off ourselves and place it on God and others. "A generous man will himself be blessed," says Proverbs 22:9. God encourages us to be bold and extravagant in our giving, not timid and tight-fisted. "Test me in this," God says, "and see if I will not throw open the floodgates of heaven and pour out so much blessing that you will not have room enough for it" (Mal. 3:10).

Nobody likes a grumpy giver, whether it's a surly server in a restaurant or a friend who, when asked to do something for you, sighs deeply and says, "Oh, all right, I'll do it, I guess. . . . " That kind of giving makes you wish you'd never asked! God reacts the same way when we give but act like it's killing us. "God loves a cheerful giver," says the apostle Paul (2 Cor. 9:7).

In today's meeting we'll look at some of the most generous people in the Bible and see what we can learn from them.

1. In a restaurant, do you like your server to be
___chatty?
___funny?
___supper-attentive, checking in constantly?
___friendly but not intrusive?
___all business?
___other:

2. What's easy for you to give away and what's difficult?

2 Corinthians 8:1-9

Paul is writing here of the gift the Macedonian Christians gave to the poor in the Jerusalem churches. He wants to encourage the church at Corinth—whose giving has slowed way down—to resume giving generously.

1. As you read this, figure out why Paul was so surprised by the giving of the Macedonians.

2. Out of what three things did the Macedonian church give (v. 2)? What would these Christians be living like if they were alive today? How would they dress? Where would they live? What struggles might they face?

3. Why does Paul stop short of "commanding" the Christians in Corinth to be more generous?

[1]And now, brothers, we want you to know about the grace that God has given the Macedonian churches. [2]Out of the most severe trial, their overflowing joy and their extreme poverty welled up in rich generosity. [3]For I testify that they gave as much as they were able, and even beyond their ability. Entirely on their own, [4]they urgently pleaded with us for the privilege of sharing in this service to the saints. [5]And they did not do as we expected, but they gave themselves first to the Lord and then to us in keeping with God's will. [6]So we urged Titus, since he had earlier made a beginning, to bring also to completion this act of grace on your part. [7]But just as you excel in everything—in faith, in speech, in knowledge, in complete earnestness and in your love for us—see that you also excel in this grace of giving.

[8]I am not commanding you, but I want to test the sincerity of your love by comparing it with the earnestness of others. [9]For you know the grace of our Lord Jesus Christ, that though he was rich, yet for your sakes he became poor, so that you through his poverty might become rich.

4. Most of us don't have a lot of money to spend on ourselves. And most of us are pretty busy people. So why should we want to give of our money and our time? What's our motivation (see vv. 7-8 for starters)?

5. How can we make our giving less of a "have to" thing and more of a willing, joyful thing? Share any suggestions that have helped you.

6. Is there an area of giving your time or money that you will think about changing as a result of today's Bible study and discussion?

Group Talk

1. In what ways do you wish you were served by your friends and classmates and families? From the group's comments you may be able to pick up a new way to serve.

2. Share an experience of being on the receiving end of someone's giving. What made the gift memorable to you?

Community

Today we begin a little study on three big words that carry a lot of freight (not fright) for God's people. The first word we'll look at is "community."

God long ago decided that some company would be nice. Being the Creator and all, God could have made anything—even the stones (see Luke 19:40)—respond with praise. But God didn't choose stones for company; God chose people. You and me. And we were created not only to be in relationship with God but also to be in relationship with others around us. Not islands of separateness but communities of togetherness. People living, working, worshiping, and playing together. One people serving one God.

Of course, God's grand plan for community was spoiled by sin. People began thinking more of themselves and less of others. They began doing things to each other that must have made God cry. But God didn't give up on people. God sent Jesus to gather a new community of believers, which we call the church. Then God sent the Holy Spirit to be with the church and to help make it one body.

God also set certain standards for living in community. We'll read about some of those standards in our Bible study today. They're high standards, not easy to attain and live by; in fact, you'll find God's people sometimes fall far short of being the kind of community they ought to be. But God says, "Keep trying! Encourage each other! Pray and worship together! Accept and welcome diversity! Serve together!"

It's worth all that and a whole lot more.

1. If you could pick any community—anyplace in the world, any group of people—in which to live for the rest of your life, which would you pick? Why?

2. Put a check by the group(s) in which you've felt close to other group members:
   ___ family
   ___ athletic team
   ___ club or other group at school
   ___ youth group at church
   ___ this Bible study group
   ___ classmates, friends at school
   ___ people at work
   ___ other:

3. The church is supposed to be a community of believers. How close do you feel to others in your congregation (10 = close like a family; 1 = distant as the moon)?

Ephesians 4:1–6, 15

¹As a prisoner for the Lord, then, I urge you to live a life worthy of the calling you have received. ²Be completely humble and gentle; be patient, bearing with one another in love. ³Make every effort to keep the unity of the Spirit through the bond of peace. ⁴There is one body and one Spirit—just as you were called to one hope when you were called—⁵one Lord, one faith, one baptism; ⁶one God and Father of all, who is over all and through all and in all. . . .

¹⁵Speaking the truth in love, we will in all things grow up into him who is the Head, that is, Christ.

Galatians 3:28

There is neither Jew nor Greek, slave nor free, male nor female, for you are all one in Christ Jesus.

1. As you read these passages, count the number of times the word "one" is used. What's the impact of all this repetition?

2. What do we have in common with all believers?

3. What's the purpose of our being in community with other believers? See verse 15 but add your own ideas as well.

4. What contrasts can you add to the list from Galatians 3:28 that would be more applicable to your high school or church (for example, neither brain nor jock . . .)?

5. Read the list in Ephesians 4:2. Which quality mentioned there is most difficult for you to practice? Share your answers with the group. Group members may say if they agree or disagree with your choice!

6. Complete this statement: One thing I personally will try to do to promote community (at school, in my home, at church) is . . .

group Talk

1. When have you felt the oneness and unity of the community of believers? Share some experiences.
2. What can we do to increase the sense of unity and community among believers at our school or church?

grace

Generally speaking, people tend to think they lead fairly good lives. For example, a person might think, *I'm not an ax murderer; I don't burn down orphanages or take candy from little kids; I don't cheat; I'm not on drugs and I don't smoke either. Besides, I go to church nearly every week and to youth group twice a month. I even get along with my parents.*

People who think this way may be telling themselves, *I'm really a pretty good person. Look at all the bad things I avoid. Look at all the good stuff I do.* All right, it *is* good not to be an ax murderer and to be kind to others. Just don't expect these things to put you right with God. Nothing we do or don't do can accomplish that.

The truth is that "all have sinned and fall short of the glory of God" (Rom. 3:23) and "the wages of sin is death" (Rom. 6:23). It's easier to swim across an ocean underwater, jump across the Grand Canyon, hold your breath for two months, or leap tall buildings in a single bound than it is to earn your own salvation.

Actually, all that grim-sounding stuff is good news for us. Why? Because we don't have to earn or deserve our salvation. It's a gift from God, given to us out of amazing grace. We latch onto that grace by faith, which is also a gift from God. Everything . . . absolutely everything . . . comes down to the wonderful grace of our God. That's the best news sinners like us will ever hear!

When you were little, maybe your parents had to remind you to say thanks for gifts ("Now, honey, what do you say to Aunt Tilly for those nice wool socks she knit you?"). We shouldn't need any reminders to live gratefully before our God, to live with a deep sense of wonder and awe at the incredible gift we've been given.

1. As a kid, what was the most impossible thing you tried to do?
   ___make up your own language
   ___build an imperishable sand castle
   ___fill a gopher hole with water
   ___make a phone line with cups and string
   ___make money selling lemonade
   ___other:

2. Did you ever receive a gift or compliment even though you didn't deserve it?

3. Have you ever felt that you were trying to win a person's approval and just weren't able to? Describe the situation.

Ephesians 2:8-9

[8]For it is by grace you have been saved, through faith—and this not from yourselves, it is the gift of God—[9]not by works, so that no one can boast.

Mark 14:66-72

[66]While Peter was below in the courtyard, one of the servant girls of the high priest came by. [67] . . . "You also were with that Nazarene, Jesus," she said.

[68]But he denied it. "I don't know or understand what you're talking about," he said, and went out into the entryway.

[69]When the servant girl saw him standing there, she said again to those standing around, "This fellow is one of them." [70]Again he denied it.

After a little while, those standing near said to Peter, "Surely you are one of them, for you are a Galilean."

[71]He began to call down curses on himself, and he swore to them, "I don't know this man you're talking about."

[72]Immediately the rooster crowed the second time. Then Peter remembered the word Jesus had spoken to him: "Before the rooster crows twice you will disown me three times." And he broke down and wept.

John 21:15

When they had finished eating, Jesus said to Simon Peter, "Simon son of John, do you truly love me more than these?"

"Yes, Lord," he said, "you know that I love you." Jesus said, "Feed my lambs."

1. As you read these passages, see how Peter treats Jesus and how Jesus responds to Peter.

2. What motivates Peter to speak as he does? Can you sympathize with his actions?

3. How does Peter respond when he realizes he has blown it? How does Jesus reinstate him?

4. Where do you see God's grace in this story?

5. Where do you see God's grace in your life? When you screw up, what do you find helpful to do?

6. What will you take with you from this passage?

Group Talk

1. God's grace towards us has been described as somewhat like our being kind to an ant. However, ants, as a general rule, don't openly rebel against us (as we do against God). Can you think of a better analogy?

2. Why would we possibly want to earn our own salvation when God wants to give it to us as a gift?

3. What should we look for in our lives to help us know that our faith is real?

START HERE →

*warm*UP

Worship

Do you ever walk out of church saying, "Man! Was that ever boring!" Have you ever sat around the Sunday dinner table and criticized the pastor or the service or both? Just about everyone, young or old, is guilty of this. Today we'll look at worship—what it really is and what our role in it can be.

"Offer your bodies as living sacrifices, holy and pleasing to God—this is your spiritual act of worship." With these words Paul begins chapter 12 of Romans. The text note on this passage calls worship "obedient service." Worship is not something God does for us; it is something we can do for God.

Sometimes we go to church thinking that we are the audience, the minister is the actor, and God is the director. Not really. It is we who are the actors, the pastor is the director, and God is the audience. We should always leave a worship service asking, How well did I worship God today? rather than, How did I like the service?

Outside of church, how we serve others is part of our worship of God. Even in the small group we're in today, we should serve each other by carrying our share of the responsibilities. By saying, "This group is boring," we might be making a statement about our own lack of responsibility.

To worship God both inside and outside of church is also to be filled with amazement and wonder at who God is and at the great things God has done. God wants—and awesomely deserves—our very best praise and adoration. "O, LORD, our LORD, how majestic is your name in all the earth!" (Ps. 8:1).

1. What's the funniest thing you've ever seen happen in a church service?

2. Think of a service you really enjoyed. What did you like about it?

3. What did Jesus do during his life that still amazes you?

Matthew 2:9-12

9After they had heard the king, they went on their way, and the star they had seen in the east went ahead of them until it stopped over the place where the child was. 10When they saw the star, they were overjoyed. 11On coming to the house, they saw the child with his mother Mary, and they bowed down and worshiped him. Then they opened their treasures and presented him with gifts of gold and of incense and of myrrh. 12And having been warned in a dream not to go back to Herod, they returned to their country by another route.

1. As you read, think about what aspects of worship are in this familiar story. Talk it over after your reading.

2. What did the wise men give Jesus?

___whatever they could scrounge along the way
___one-tenth of their possessions
___the best they had
___gifts fit for a king

3. What one word in the Scripture passage (besides "worship") captures the wise men's reaction to the baby Jesus? How important is that word to our worship, do you think?

4. Compare these aspects of the wise men's worship to our worship today (in other words, what do we do in our worship in and out of church that's like these things?):

- expending a great deal of effort to find the Lord
- being "overjoyed" at finding him
- bowing down and worshiping him
- presenting gifts to him

5. What have you left behind to pursue Jesus?

___your country
___your money
___your security
___your chia pet
___what!?

6. Express a little of your own wonder at who God is and what God has done. If you wish, use a prayer format for your praise and thanks: "Dear God, I praise and thank you for . . . "

group Talk

1. Explain how you are going to bite your tongue when you're about to say something critical about church next (or any) Sunday.
2. When you go to church, do you feel more like "the audience" or "the actors"? Explain.
3. How can we make worship more a part of our daily lives?